RÉUNION ISLAND TRAVEL GUIDE 2026

Adventures and Cultural Gems in the Indian Ocean

William P. Baker

Copyright

Copyright 2025 William P. Baker. All rights reserved.

No part of this publication may be reproduced, distributed, or transmitted in any form or by any means, including photocopying, recording, or other electronic or mechanical methods, without the prior written permission of the copyright owner.

Table of content

Introduction
    My visit to Réunion Island
Chapter 1
    Preparing for Your Trip
        When to Visit
        Entry Requirements and Travel Documents
        Health, Vaccinations, and Travel Insurance
        Currency, Banking, and Payment Tips
        Packing Smart for the Island
Chapter 2
    Getting to and Around Réunion Island
        International Flights and Airlines Serving Réunion
        Arrival at Roland Garros Airport
        Public Transportation
        Renting a Car and Driving Tips
        Eco-friendly Ways to Explore the Island
Chapter 3
    Understanding Réunion Island
        A Short History of the Island
        Languages and Communication Essentials
        Religion and Traditions in Everyday Life
        Festivals and Annual Celebrations
        Arts, Music, and Local Crafts
Chapter 4
    Laws, Safety, and Visitor Rights
        Local Laws Every Visitor Should Know
        Safety Tips in Cities, Villages, and Remote Areas
        Rules for Hiking and Nature Conservation
        Emergency Services and Useful Numbers
        Respectful Behavior and Cultural Etiquette

Chapter 5
Where to Stay
- Luxury Resorts on the Coast
- Budget-friendly Hotels and Guesthouses
- Charming Bed and Breakfasts
- Mountain Lodges and Gîtes in the Cirques
- Unique Stays

Chapter 6
Food and Culinary Experiences
- Traditional Creole Cuisine Explained
- Street Food and Local Snacks to Try
- Fresh Market Finds: Fruits, Spices, and Coffee
- Fine Dining and French Influences
- Rum, Sugarcane, and Island Drinks

Chapter 7
Top Attractions and Natural Wonders
- Piton de la Fournaise
- The Three Cirques
- Black and White Sand Beaches of the West Coast
- Waterfalls, Rivers, and Natural Pools
- Botanical Gardens and Nature Parks

Chapter 8
Outdoor Adventures and Activities
- Hiking Trails for All Levels
- Paragliding and Aerial Views of the Island
- Scuba Diving, Snorkeling, and Marine Life
- Whale Watching and Dolphin Tours
- Canyoning and Mountain Sports

Chapter 9
Shopping, Entertainment, and Nightlife
- Souvenir Shopping and Local Handicrafts
- Colorful Markets and What to Buy
- Shopping Centers and Modern Boutiques

Nightlife in Saint Gilles and Saint Denis
  Cultural Shows and Sega Music Nights
Chapter 10
  Practical Tips for a Smooth Stay
    Internet, Mobile Service, and Staying Connected
    Public Holidays and How They Affect Travel
    Budgeting and Average Daily Costs
    Accessibility for Travelers with Disabilities
    Departure Tips and Last-minute Essentials
Conclusion

SCAN THE QR CODE

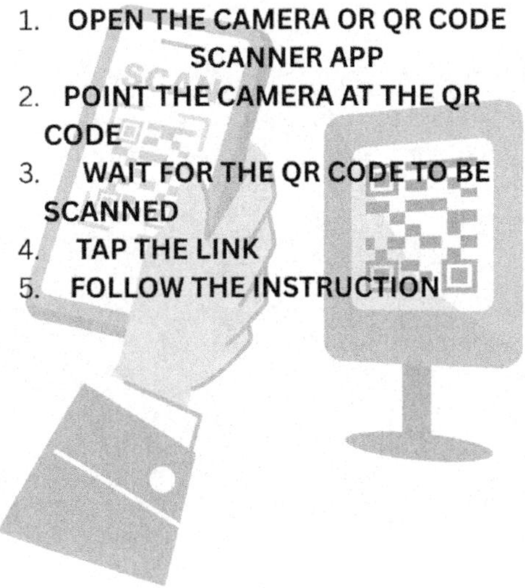

1. OPEN THE CAMERA OR QR CODE SCANNER APP
2. POINT THE CAMERA AT THE QR CODE
3. WAIT FOR THE QR CODE TO BE SCANNED
4. TAP THE LINK
5. FOLLOW THE INSTRUCTION

SCAN HERE

Introduction

My visit to Réunion Island

The first time I set foot on Réunion Island, I felt as though I had landed in a place that carried both mystery and warmth in equal measure. The air was filled with the scent of frangipani mixed with the salty breeze of the Indian Ocean, and the island's rugged beauty pulled me in before I had even collected my bags. I had heard about this small French territory far out in the ocean, but no description had prepared me for the striking mix of cultures, the dramatic landscapes, and the simple joy of moving from beach to mountain in the same day.

My most memorable days on the island began in the capital, Saint Denis. The city itself is not where people often linger, but I found the blend of Creole architecture, lively markets, and French cafés fascinating. Walking through the streets, I heard French, Creole, Malagasy, and Tamil spoken almost in the same breath. At the market, I was drawn toward tables stacked with bright red lychees, bunches of bananas still on their stalks, and spices that carried a fragrance strong enough to cling to my clothes. I tried samoussas, small golden pastries filled with spiced meat or vegetables, and was struck by how easily flavors from India, Africa, and Europe came together on this island.

Leaving the capital behind, I drove along winding roads that hugged the coastline before climbing toward the heart of the island. The road twisted through sugarcane fields that stretched endlessly, and the further I went, the more I realized why Réunion is known as a paradise for hikers and nature lovers. At the center of the island lies the Cirque de Salazie, a vast amphitheater of green mountains carved by ancient volcanic activity. It was here that I stayed in a small guesthouse run by a Creole family. They welcomed me with rum infused with local spices and served a dinner of cari, a traditional stew of chicken cooked slowly with turmeric and thyme.

The flavors were bold yet comforting, and the conversation around the table made me feel less like a tourist and more like a guest of the island.

From Salazie I continued on to the Cirque de Mafate, a place that can only be reached on foot or by helicopter. The trail began with a steady climb, and I quickly understood why locals speak of Mafate with a kind of reverence. As I hiked deeper into the cirque, waterfalls spilled down sheer cliffs, and tiny villages appeared like hidden secrets among the folds of the mountains. There was no traffic here, no sound of engines, only the rhythm of footsteps and the laughter of children who ran along paths barefoot. Spending a night in a gîte, or mountain lodge, I realized how rare it is today to be somewhere completely cut off from the rush of modern life. The stars over Mafate seemed brighter, and the silence had a weight to it that was almost spiritual.

The island's volcanic side offered another unforgettable experience. Piton de la Fournaise, one of the most active volcanoes in the world, was unlike anything I had ever seen. I woke before dawn to join a group trek across its barren slopes. At first the ground was black and cracked, like a landscape frozen in fire, but as the sun rose, the surface glowed in shades of red and gold. Each step felt as if I were walking on the skin of the earth itself. Though it was demanding, the climb to the crater rim rewarded me with a view that is difficult to put into words. The scale of the caldera, the steam rising from fissures, and the sense of standing on something so alive made me feel both small and privileged to witness it.

Of course, no story of Réunion is complete without mentioning its beaches. After days of hiking, I longed for the sea, and I found myself drawn to the western coast where the lagoon stretched calm and clear. In Saint Gilles, I rented a mask and snorkel and drifted among corals where parrotfish and angelfish glided past with ease. The water was warm, and the reef protected the shore from strong currents, making it a peaceful spot to spend the afternoon. At sunset, the sky turned shades of orange and purple, and families gathered on the sand while local musicians played sega, the traditional music of the island, on drums and guitars. It was the kind of moment that imprints itself permanently in memory.

What made my time in Réunion most special, however, was not only the natural beauty but the way the island seemed to embrace diversity. In one day I could share breakfast of French croissants, lunch of Creole rougail saucisse, and dinner of Tamil curry served with rice. Churches stood near Hindu temples, and mosques echoed not far from Chinese pagodas. Festivals celebrated with drums and dance brought people from different backgrounds together with a sense of ease that felt rare. There was no single identity here, but rather a harmony created from many roots.

When it came time to leave, I sat on the balcony of my guesthouse overlooking the sea and thought about what I would carry home. It was not only the memory of the volcano or the quiet nights in Mafate but the realization that an island so small could hold such vast contrasts and still remain balanced. My time in Réunion taught me that travel is not only about what you see but about how a place reshapes the way you think. The island left me with a deeper respect for nature's power, a richer understanding of culture, and the reminder that some of the most memorable journeys are the ones that surprise you the most.

Even now, long after my plane lifted off from Roland Garros Airport, I can still hear the rhythm of sega music in my head and still taste the warmth of Creole spices. Réunion was not just a destination, it was an experience that stayed with me, layered with sights, sounds, and flavors that I will never forget.

Chapter 1

Preparing for Your Trip

When to Visit

The timing of a trip to Réunion Island makes a big difference in how much you enjoy the experience. The island has a tropical climate, yet it does not feel uniform throughout the year. Each season carries its own character, shaping what travelers can do and what they will see. From beach holidays to mountain hikes, the rhythm of the year on Réunion is a guide in itself.

The period from May to November is the dry season and is widely considered the best time to visit. The days are clear, the skies bright, and the humidity lower than at other times of the year. Temperatures during these months stay comfortable, averaging between 20 and 25 degrees Celsius along the coast, while the mountain areas remain cooler. This is also when hiking conditions are at their finest. Trails in the cirques of Mafate, Salazie, and Cilaos stay firm and safe, waterfalls are full but not overwhelming, and the chances of storms are low. For anyone wanting to explore Piton de la Fournaise, this period gives the highest chance of calm weather and good visibility. Hotels and guesthouses are usually busier from July to September because many French visitors travel during their summer holidays, so booking in advance is recommended if you are coming in those months.

From December to April, Réunion experiences its wet season. During this time, the island becomes lush and intensely green, but the rain can be heavy and frequent. Humidity rises, and temperatures along the coast reach an average of 28 to 30 degrees Celsius. This is also cyclone season, and while not every year sees direct impacts, the risk is present. Roads can close because of landslides, and hiking trails may become dangerous. On the other hand, the wet season has its advantages. The waterfalls reach their most spectacular flow, markets are rich with seasonal fruits like mangoes and lychees, and accommodation prices are often lower. Travelers who enjoy quieter towns and cheaper stays may find this season appealing, provided they plan carefully and remain flexible.

Whale watching adds another layer to the calendar. From June to October, humpback whales travel through the warm waters off the coast of Réunion. Boat tours depart from Saint Gilles and Saint Leu, offering the chance to see these giants up close. Prices for tours range from 40 to 70 euros per person, depending on the operator and the type of boat used. These excursions usually start in the morning and last about three to four hours, giving visitors time to also enjoy the beaches later in the day.

Events and festivals can also shape the best time to visit. In January, the Tamil community celebrates Cavadee with colorful processions and rituals that reveal the depth of cultural diversity on the island. In July, the Festival Liberté Métisse in Saint Paul celebrates the island's history and traditions with music, dance, and food, creating a lively atmosphere. Around October or November, the Dipavali festival brings light and color to the towns as part of the Hindu calendar. These events not only provide entertainment but also give visitors a chance to experience local traditions that go beyond sightseeing.

Beach lovers will appreciate that the lagoon on the west coast remains warm throughout the year, with water temperatures ranging between 23 and 28 degrees Celsius. While the dry season offers calm seas and perfect snorkeling, the wet months can still provide enjoyable swimming, especially within protected areas like the beaches of L'Hermitage and La Saline. Restaurants and bars along the coast stay open year-round, with peak activity during the European holiday season from July to August and again in December.

Those planning hikes in the highlands should note that early mornings are the most rewarding, regardless of season. Clouds tend to gather by midday, especially in the cirques, so starting trails at sunrise gives the best chance for views and photographs. There is no entrance fee for hiking trails, but if you wish to join guided tours, prices average from 50 to 90 euros per day, with departure points often arranged in Saint Denis or Saint Pierre.

When weighing the best time to visit, the dry season remains the most practical choice for first-time visitors, offering both safety and variety in activities. The wet season has its own charm, but it demands more patience and adaptability. In both periods, Réunion rewards travelers with scenery and culture that cannot be matched elsewhere. Whether for hiking, whale watching, cultural festivals, or simply enjoying a warm stretch of sand, the island provides a calendar full of reasons to come. The most important step is to match the season with your interests and prepare accordingly, so every day feels like time well spent.

Entry Requirements and Travel Documents

Travelers heading to Réunion Island need to keep in mind that this French overseas department follows the same entry rules as mainland France. Citizens of the European Union and the Schengen area can arrive with a valid national identity card or passport and do not need a visa for their stay. For visitors from countries outside of Europe, a valid passport is required, and in most cases a French visa will be necessary. Some nationalities are exempt from a visa for short stays of up to ninety days, but travelers should check carefully with the nearest French consulate or embassy before making plans. The visa granted for France and the Schengen area also covers Réunion, but a Schengen visa marked as valid only for Europe does not automatically apply to the island, so travelers must ensure their visa specifically mentions French overseas territories.

On arrival at Roland Garros International Airport in Saint Denis, border controls are carried out in the same manner as in France. Immigration officers will request to see a passport or identity card along with any visa if required. Proof of onward travel and accommodation bookings may also be asked for, especially if you are not a European citizen. Customs checks follow French law, which means strict controls on the import of certain foods, plants, and animal products. Duty free allowances are in line with those in France, so travelers can bring in limited quantities of alcohol and tobacco without paying extra fees.

For longer stays, students, workers, and those joining family will need to apply for the appropriate long stay visa before travel. This process involves submitting application forms, photographs, proof of accommodation, and in some cases medical certificates. Fees vary depending on the type of visa, but for short stay visas the cost is generally around eighty euros. Applications are made at French consulates, and processing times can take several weeks, so planning well in advance is important.

Health insurance is strongly advised. European travelers holding a European Health Insurance Card can use it in Réunion, but it is recommended to also carry private travel insurance for full coverage, especially if you plan outdoor activities such as hiking, canyoning, or scuba diving. Non European visitors should always carry comprehensive insurance that includes medical evacuation, as the cost of treatment and transfers can be high.

Children traveling with parents or guardians must have their own passport or identity card, as France does not allow minors to be listed on a parent's document. If a child is traveling without one or both parents, written authorization from the absent parent or guardian may be required. This authorization should be notarized or officially certified to avoid problems at immigration.

It is also wise to carry copies of all documents. Photocopies stored separately from the originals, or digital copies saved securely, can save a great deal of trouble if a passport is lost. In such cases, travelers should contact their embassy or consulate in France, as Réunion itself does not host foreign embassies. The local police in Saint Denis can issue a report for lost or stolen documents, which will be needed to obtain temporary travel papers.

Stays longer than ninety days require registration with the French Office of Immigration and Integration. This involves medical checks and administrative steps that must be completed within three months of arrival. Addresses and office times are available in Saint Denis, and it is essential not to miss these appointments to keep your stay legal.

The island's airports and seaports operate under French regulations, with Roland Garros Airport open daily for international arrivals. Opening hours of consulates in mainland countries vary, so travelers should check before visiting to submit visa applications. French embassies abroad usually handle appointments in the morning, with offices often closed in the afternoon. Visa fees are paid at the time of application, and receipts should be kept for reference.

By ensuring passports are valid for at least six months after travel dates, checking visa needs early, and carrying insurance, visitors can arrive in Réunion with peace of mind. Entry procedures are efficient, but only if documents are in order. Those who prepare well in advance will find that passing through immigration is straightforward, allowing more time to focus on enjoying the island itself.

Health, Vaccinations, and Travel Insurance

Travelers to Réunion Island will find that health standards are high, with medical facilities meeting the same level of care as in mainland France. There is no requirement for compulsory vaccinations to enter the island, but it is advisable to be up to date with common immunizations such as tetanus, hepatitis A, hepatitis B, typhoid, and measles. For those planning extended stays in rural areas or engaging in outdoor activities, a doctor may also recommend protection against rabies, even though the risk is relatively low. The island has a tropical climate and mosquito borne illnesses such as dengue fever and chikungunya occasionally appear, so prevention measures like insect repellent, long clothing in the evening, and mosquito nets remain practical steps for travelers.

Pharmacies are easy to find in towns such as Saint Denis, Saint Gilles, and Saint Pierre, with recognizable green crosses marking their location. They open from Monday to Saturday, generally from 8.30 in the morning until 6.30 in the evening, though many close for a few hours at midday. In larger towns at least one pharmacy stays open overnight or on Sundays, with the location posted on the doors of local shops and medical offices. Pharmacies sell mosquito repellent, sunscreen, over the counter medicine, and can provide advice for minor ailments. For serious issues, hospitals such as Groupe Hospitalier Est Réunion in Saint Benoît and Centre Hospitalier Universitaire in Saint Denis offer emergency and specialist care.

Medical services on the island can be costly for travelers without insurance. A consultation with a private doctor may cost between 25 and 40 euros, while treatment in a hospital can be significantly more. European travelers with a European Health Insurance Card can use public hospitals under the same conditions as French citizens, but private insurance is still strongly advised to cover all expenses. For non European visitors, comprehensive travel insurance that includes medical care and evacuation is essential, especially for activities in remote mountain areas. Policies should also cover adventure sports if you plan to go hiking in the cirques, canyoning in rivers, or paragliding over the coast. Insurance packages vary, but basic plans usually start from around 30 euros per week, while extended coverage with evacuation can range from 70 to 100 euros per week.

Mosquito protection is particularly important in the warmer months. Dengue fever cases tend to increase during the rainy season between

December and April. There is no vaccine available for most travelers, so preventive measures are the best defense. Using repellent that contains DEET or icaridin, wearing light long sleeved clothing, and sleeping under nets in rural areas greatly reduces risk. Most hotels and guesthouses provide nets and often spray rooms regularly, but carrying your own repellent ensures constant protection.

Tap water in Réunion is safe to drink in towns and hotels, though visitors hiking in the mountains should not drink directly from streams without purification tablets or filters, as rainfall can affect water quality. Bottled water is widely available and costs about one euro for a 1.5 liter bottle in supermarkets.

For emergencies, dial 15 for medical help, 17 for police, and 18 for fire and rescue. Ambulance services are reliable and quick to respond, particularly in urban areas. In more remote zones, helicopters are often used to evacuate patients, which is another reason insurance covering medical transport is vital.

Dentists, general practitioners, and specialists such as dermatologists and pediatricians are available across the island, usually by appointment. Most clinics operate during the week from 8 in the morning to 5 in the afternoon. Some doctors offer consultations in English, but French is the main language spoken in medical settings. Having your insurance documents and identification ready makes the process smoother.

With a little preparation, health concerns need not interrupt your trip. Keeping vaccinations current, using mosquito protection, drinking safe water, and carrying solid insurance ensures that your time on Réunion can be spent enjoying the island rather than worrying about medical issues. The health system is reliable, but being prepared will give you confidence to explore every corner of the island without unnecessary stress.

Currency, Banking, and Payment Tips

The official currency in Réunion Island is the euro, which makes transactions straightforward for travelers arriving from Europe. Coins and notes are the same as those used in mainland France, so visitors carrying euros from elsewhere in the Eurozone can use them without difficulty. Prices on the island are slightly higher than in mainland France because of transport costs, but still reasonable compared to many island destinations. A simple Creole meal at a local eatery may cost around ten to twelve euros, while a coffee averages two euros in a café.

Banks are located in all major towns, with branches of Crédit Agricole, BNP Paribas, and Société Générale widely available. They usually open from Monday to Friday between 8.30 in the morning and 4.00 in the afternoon, with some branches open on Saturday mornings until midday. Most banks close during lunch hours, and they are not open on Sundays or public holidays. ATMs are attached to most branches and are also found in shopping centers, supermarkets, and tourist zones such as Saint Denis, Saint Pierre, and Saint Gilles. These machines accept international cards from Visa and MasterCard, dispensing cash in euros at the daily exchange rate. Withdrawals may carry small fees depending on your bank, so checking with your provider before travel is helpful.

Credit and debit cards are widely accepted in hotels, restaurants, and larger shops, with contactless payment available in many places. Smaller family run establishments, market stalls, and rural guesthouses may prefer cash, so carrying a mix of notes and coins is recommended. Some gîtes in the mountain cirques operate on a cash only basis, so travelers planning overnight stays in Mafate or Salazie should withdraw money in advance in coastal towns. Daily withdrawal limits at ATMs are usually between 300 and 500 euros, which is enough for most expenses.

Currency exchange services are available at Roland Garros International Airport and in major towns, though the rates are often less favorable than those offered by withdrawing directly from ATMs. For visitors arriving without euros, it is practical to change a small amount at the airport for immediate expenses such as taxis, then rely on bank machines for better rates. Exchange offices in Saint Denis are usually open during business hours, often from 9.00 in the morning until 5.00 in the evening.

Tipping is not obligatory in Réunion, as service charges are included in bills by law, but it is appreciated for good service. Rounding up the bill or leaving an extra euro or two in cafés and taxis is common. In fine dining restaurants, leaving around five to ten percent of the total is customary if the service is excellent.

Budget planning helps visitors enjoy their trip without stress. On average, budget travelers may spend around fifty to seventy euros per day when staying in simple guesthouses and eating at local restaurants. Mid range travelers should expect daily expenses between one hundred and one hundred fifty euros, covering comfortable hotels, rental cars, and a mix of dining options. Those choosing luxury resorts and guided tours may spend upwards of two hundred euros per day.

Most supermarkets and shops accept card payments without a minimum charge, though local markets often ask for cash. Market days are lively and worth experiencing, with fruit, spices, and souvenirs available at fair prices. A bag of fresh lychees costs around five euros in season, while handwoven baskets or artisanal crafts vary between ten and twenty euros. Carrying small change is useful when shopping in these places.

By knowing where to access money, carrying some cash for remote areas, and using cards for larger transactions, visitors will find managing finances on Réunion Island straightforward. With reliable banks, ATMs in convenient locations, and prices clearly displayed in euros, spending on the island is simple and secure, allowing more time to enjoy the beaches, mountains, and vibrant markets without concern.

Packing Smart for the Island

Packing for Réunion Island calls for balance, since the island offers both sunny beaches and rugged volcanic landscapes. Lightweight clothing is essential for the warm coastal areas, with breathable shirts, shorts, and dresses keeping you comfortable in the tropical heat. Swimwear is a must for lagoon days and hotel pools, and a light cover-up helps when strolling through town or visiting markets. A hat, sunglasses, and high protection sunscreen will make long afternoons under the sun far more pleasant, especially as the island's rays are strong year round.

For the highlands and the cirques, the weather shifts quickly, so layering is key. Early mornings in places like Cilaos or Salazie can feel chilly, dropping to around ten degrees Celsius, while afternoons warm up considerably. A fleece or light sweater paired with a waterproof jacket is enough to handle the cooler air and the sudden rain showers common in the mountains. Comfortable walking trousers and breathable socks are recommended for hiking trails, along with sturdy shoes that grip well on rocky or muddy paths. Hiking boots can be bought locally in Saint Denis or Saint Pierre, but prices are higher than in Europe, so bringing your own pair is more practical.

Rain showers are frequent, especially between December and April, so a compact umbrella or lightweight raincoat makes moving through towns and trails much easier. For travelers staying near the coast, sandals or flip flops are convenient, but water shoes are helpful if you plan to explore rocky beaches or natural pools. Snorkeling gear is available for rent in Saint Gilles or Saint Leu, with daily rates around five to ten euros, though many visitors prefer to pack their own mask and fins for comfort.

Mosquito protection should not be overlooked. Repellent, preferably containing DEET or icaridin, is important during the wet season when mosquitoes are more active. Pharmacies across the island stock sprays and lotions, with prices starting around six euros, but carrying your own ensures you have it from the start. After sun cream or aloe vera gel also comes in handy after long hours outdoors.

Power outlets in Réunion follow the European two pin system, with a standard voltage of 220 volts. Travelers from outside Europe should bring a universal adapter to charge phones, cameras, and laptops. Mobile signal is strong across most of the island, though service can fade in remote parts of Mafate. A portable charger will keep devices working during long treks, especially when you rely on your phone for navigation.

Daypacks are useful for both beach outings and mountain hikes. A small backpack that holds a bottle of water, snacks, a light jacket, and sunscreen will serve you well during daily activities. Bottled water is inexpensive at supermarkets, usually one euro for a large bottle, but a reusable water bottle is more convenient and eco friendly. Shops in Saint Denis and Saint Pierre also sell water filters and tablets if you plan to drink from mountain streams during hikes.

In addition to clothing and gear, carrying a small first aid kit is always wise. Basic items such as bandages, antiseptic cream, and pain relief tablets are easy to pack and will save you from unexpected trips to the pharmacy. Those with prescription medicine should bring enough for the trip, along with copies of prescriptions in case replacements are needed.

With a suitcase that combines beachwear, mountain gear, and a few practical extras, you will be well equipped for every part of Réunion. Packing with care allows you to adapt to the sudden changes in weather, the mix of activities, and the blend of urban and natural settings. By preparing thoughtfully, you will be ready to enjoy the rhythm of the island without needing to rush for forgotten essentials.

Chapter 2

Getting to and Around Réunion Island

International Flights and Airlines Serving Réunion

Reaching Réunion Island is straightforward thanks to regular international connections that link the island with Europe, Africa, and nearby islands in the Indian Ocean. The main gateway is Roland Garros Airport, located in Sainte Marie about ten kilometers from Saint Denis. This airport handles most international arrivals and operates daily, with services running from early morning until late evening. Facilities include car rental counters, restaurants, shops, and currency exchange, all open in line with flight schedules.

From mainland France, several airlines provide direct flights. Air France, Air Austral, and Corsair fly regularly from Paris, with departures from both Charles de Gaulle and Orly airports. Flights typically take around eleven hours non stop, and prices vary according to the season. A return ticket in the low season can start at around 600 euros, while peak season fares often climb to 900 euros or more. Air Austral, based in Réunion, offers additional comfort with seasonal promotions and packages that include onward connections to Mauritius, Madagascar, and Mayotte.

For travelers coming from Africa, Air Austral and Air Madagascar link Réunion with Antananarivo, while Air Mauritius connects with Port Louis several times a week. These shorter regional flights usually take less than two hours, making it easy to combine a trip to Réunion with visits to neighboring islands. South African Airways and Air Austral also maintain services from Johannesburg, opening the island to travelers from southern Africa. Average fares on these routes range from 250 to 400 euros return, depending on availability and season.

Connections from Asia and the Middle East are available through stopovers. Emirates flies from Dubai to Réunion with a daily service, offering convenient links for passengers coming from Asia, the Middle East, or Australia. The route takes around seven hours, and fares generally begin at 700 euros return. This service has expanded options for international visitors who prefer not to connect through Paris.

Regional airlines also operate flights between Réunion and other French territories in the Indian Ocean. Air Austral connects to Mayotte several times a week, with flight times of around two hours. Prices average between 200 and 350 euros return, and these routes are popular with both tourists and local residents.

The airport is modern and well organized, with services adapted to international travelers. Taxi stands are located just outside the arrivals hall, and fares to Saint Denis usually cost around 25 euros during the day, slightly more at night. Buses also connect the airport with the city, departing every hour during the day with a fare of about 2 euros. Car rental desks open daily from 7.00 in the morning until 10.00 at night, giving visitors flexible options on arrival.

When booking flights, it is worth noting that prices increase significantly during the French school holidays, particularly in July, August, and December. Seats sell quickly in these periods, so reserving months ahead is advisable. Travelers who prefer lower fares and quieter flights may find the shoulder seasons of May to June and September to November more comfortable, with tickets easier to secure and fewer crowds at the airport.

With reliable carriers, regular schedules, and a well equipped airport, arriving in Réunion is smooth. Whether flying direct from Europe or connecting through Africa or the Middle East, the journey is efficient, allowing visitors to start enjoying the island's mix of mountains, beaches, and Creole culture without unnecessary delays.

Arrival at Roland Garros Airport

Arriving at Roland Garros Airport in Sainte Marie places you just a short drive from Saint Denis and serves as the first glimpse of how smoothly the island welcomes its visitors. The airport is compact but efficient, handling both long haul flights from Paris and regional services across the Indian Ocean. Immigration procedures follow French regulations, and the lines usually move quickly, though peak arrivals from Europe in the early morning can bring a longer wait. Having travel documents ready makes the process simple, and baggage claim areas are located just after passport control with clear signs in French and English.

Once through customs, the arrivals hall offers a range of services. Currency exchange counters are open in line with international flight schedules, though withdrawing euros directly from the ATMs in the terminal often gives better rates. Car rental agencies such as Europcar, Hertz, and local operators keep desks near the exit, with opening hours from 7.00 in the morning until 10.00 at night. Pre booking is strongly advised in high season, as vehicles sell out quickly. Daily rates for small cars start at around 30 euros, with four wheel drives and vans costing more depending on demand.

For travelers heading into Saint Denis, taxis wait outside the arrivals area throughout the day and night. A daytime ride to the city center costs around 25 euros, with a slight surcharge after 8.00 in the evening. If you are going farther south to Saint Gilles or Saint Pierre, fares increase to 70 or 90 euros depending on distance. Buses also connect the airport with Saint Denis, operating during the day at hourly intervals. The fare is about 2 euros and tickets can be bought directly from the driver. Shuttle services run by hotels and tour operators are another option, usually arranged in advance with pick up points just outside the terminal.

Inside the airport, cafés and snack bars serve light meals, pastries, and coffee, while souvenir shops sell rum, vanilla, and local crafts. Prices are slightly higher than in town, so many travelers prefer to wait until they reach Saint Denis or the markets. Free Wi Fi is available in the terminal, and seating areas are spacious enough for those waiting for connecting flights. Duty free stores open alongside international departures, offering spirits, perfume, and chocolates at competitive rates.

The airport operates daily, with most international flights arriving early in the morning and departures scheduled later in the day. Check in counters open three hours before departure, and security checks are thorough but efficient. For regional flights to nearby islands such as Mauritius or Madagascar, check in is usually required two hours before boarding.

Roland Garros Airport is not large, so moving from one area to another takes only a few minutes. This makes connections straightforward, and announcements in both French and English keep travelers informed. Seating is comfortable, and staff are generally helpful with directions. There are medical services available in case of emergencies, as well as information desks that stay open during all operating hours.

For those with early flights or late arrivals, several hotels are located within ten minutes of the airport. Rates start at around 60 euros per night for mid range options, with check in times usually from 2.00 in the afternoon and check out around 11.00 in the morning. Many of these hotels provide shuttle transfers on request.

Arrival at Roland Garros Airport sets the tone for the rest of your journey. The process is organized, the facilities are modern, and the onward travel options make it easy to start exploring Réunion right away, whether you are bound for the capital, the beaches of the west coast, or the mountains at the heart of the island.

Public Transportation

Public transportation in Réunion Island is reliable for reaching towns along the coast and provides an affordable way to move around without renting a car. The network is based on buses, which are operated mainly by Car Jaune, easily recognized by their yellow color. These buses link Saint Denis, Saint Pierre, Saint Gilles, and other major towns, running daily from early morning until around 7.00 in the evening. Fares are inexpensive, starting from about 2 euros for shorter routes and rising to 5 or 6 euros for longer journeys across the island. Tickets can be purchased directly from the driver or at bus stations, and most vehicles accept contactless card payments as well as cash.

In Saint Denis, the main station is located on Rue de la Gare, where buses depart for different parts of the island. Car Jaune routes cover the airport, the western coast resorts, and the southern towns, with schedules posted at stops and online. Travel times can be lengthy because of traffic, especially during rush hours between 7.00 and 9.00 in the morning and again from 4.00 to 6.00 in the evening. However, buses are air conditioned, comfortable, and a good way to see the landscape while moving from one destination to another.

Regional buses known as Cars Régionaux provide access to smaller villages and mountain towns such as Cilaos and Salazie. These routes are slower and less frequent, often running only a few times a day, so checking timetables in advance is essential. For example, the road to Cilaos includes more than 400 bends, so trips take longer than expected, but the scenery along the way is worth the ride. Fares for these regional lines usually range from 3 to 8 euros depending on the distance.

Taxis are available in all main towns, but they are more expensive than buses. A short trip within Saint Denis can cost around 10 euros, while a journey from the airport to the city center is about 25 euros. Prices increase for longer distances, and it is common to pay 80 to 90 euros to reach Saint Gilles or Saint Pierre. Taxi stands are found at airports, bus terminals, and major hotels, and drivers use meters, although it is wise to confirm the fare before starting the trip.

Shared minibuses, often called taxis collectifs, operate in certain areas and provide a practical option when buses are not running. They usually depart once full, connecting towns at lower prices than regular taxis. These vehicles are not bound to strict schedules, but they are useful for early morning departures or late returns when standard buses have stopped running.

For travelers who want to use public transportation exclusively, planning is important. Services do not always cover remote hiking trailheads, so reaching places like Mafate often requires a combination of buses and taxis. Still, for coastal towns and local markets, the bus network remains the most economical and convenient option. With clear routes, low prices, and dependable service during the day, public transportation makes exploring Réunion accessible without needing to drive.

Renting a Car and Driving Tips

Renting a car in Réunion Island is often the best way to explore freely, as public transportation does not always reach remote trails, mountain villages, or hidden beaches. Car rental desks are available at Roland Garros Airport in Sainte Marie, with well known international companies such as Europcar, Hertz, and Avis alongside local operators. They usually open daily from 7.00 in the morning until 10.00 at night, with some offices adjusting their hours to match flight arrivals. Prices for small economy cars start around 30 euros per day, rising to 50 or more for larger vehicles. Four wheel drives are popular for those planning to explore rugged mountain roads, with rates averaging 70 to 90 euros daily. Booking in advance is recommended during school holidays, particularly in July, August, and December when demand is high.

Driving in Réunion follows French rules, with traffic on the right side of the road and roundabouts giving priority to vehicles already inside. Roads are generally well maintained along the coast, but mountain routes can be narrow and winding. The drive to Cilaos is a prime example, with hundreds of sharp bends and steep sections that require patience and confidence. Allow extra time for these routes, and avoid rushing, as locals are accustomed to the roads and may drive faster than visitors. Speed limits are clearly marked, usually 50 km per hour in towns, 80 km per hour on main roads, and up to 110 km per hour on dual carriageways. Fines for speeding are strict and can be costly, so keeping within limits is important.

Fuel stations are plentiful in major towns and along main highways. Most stations open from 6.00 in the morning until 8.00 in the evening, though some in larger towns remain open later. Prices are similar to mainland France, with unleaded petrol averaging around 1.70 euros per liter. In smaller villages, stations may close for lunch breaks or Sundays, so filling up in advance is a wise precaution. Payment at stations can be made by card or cash, and many accept contactless payments.

Parking in cities like Saint Denis and Saint Pierre can be tricky during the day, as spaces fill quickly. Pay and display meters are common, charging around 1.50 to 2 euros per hour, with free parking in the evenings and on Sundays. In coastal resorts such as Saint Gilles, free parking lots are located near the beaches, though they can be busy in the afternoons. Mountain towns often have small public car parks, with no fees required.

Seat belts are mandatory for all passengers, and children under ten must use appropriate car seats. It is also worth noting that alcohol limits for drivers are lower than in some countries, at 0.5 grams per liter of blood. Random checks are frequent, especially at night and on weekends, so it is best to avoid drinking when driving altogether.

Many visitors choose to rent GPS units, though using a smartphone with offline maps works just as well, as signal is generally reliable except in parts of Mafate where cars cannot reach anyway. Renting through larger agencies often includes basic insurance, but checking the details of coverage is essential, particularly regarding excess charges. Additional insurance can reduce the risk of high costs in case of damage, with prices starting around 10 euros per day.

Having a car allows access to some of the island's finest experiences, from reaching the trailhead to Piton de la Fournaise before sunrise to exploring quiet fishing villages on the south coast. The freedom to stop at viewpoints, visit remote waterfalls, and adjust your pace makes driving a rewarding part of the journey. With careful planning, respect for road conditions, and a well chosen vehicle, renting a car in Réunion adds comfort and flexibility that makes exploring the island far easier and more enjoyable.

Eco-friendly Ways to Explore the Island

Exploring Réunion Island in eco friendly ways is both rewarding and practical, since the island's landscapes are best experienced at a slower pace that respects the environment. One of the most popular methods is hiking, as the island is covered with trails that link coastal towns to volcanic peaks and lush cirques. Paths are well marked and maintained, with access free of charge throughout the year. Local guides offer tours for those who want deeper insight into flora, fauna, and cultural history, with prices starting around 40 euros per person for half day walks. Early mornings are the best time to set out, as the weather is cooler and mountain views clearer.

Cycling is another sustainable option, with roads around Saint Denis and the west coast suited to casual riders, while more experienced cyclists can test themselves on the steep ascents toward Cilaos or Maïdo. Rentals are available in Saint Gilles and Saint Pierre, with daily rates beginning at 20 euros for standard bikes and 40 euros for electric models that make climbs more manageable. Shops usually open from 8.00 in the morning until 6.00 in the evening, and many provide helmets, locks, and repair kits as part of the rental.

Public buses, particularly the Car Jaune network, are an affordable and environmentally conscious way to reach most towns. Fares cost between 2 and 5 euros depending on distance, and services run from early morning until early evening. While buses may not reach remote mountain areas, they reduce car use on the busier coastal roads and allow travelers to experience daily life alongside local residents.

Car sharing services have also gained popularity on the island, offering an alternative to renting vehicles individually. Platforms allow travelers to book seats in cars already making journeys between towns, reducing fuel consumption and costs. Fares are usually less than half the price of a standard taxi, and meeting points are arranged in advance at bus stations or supermarkets.

Eco tours focused on marine life provide another way to travel responsibly. In Saint Gilles and Saint Leu, operators run whale and dolphin watching trips with strict codes of conduct to protect the animals. Prices range from 40 to 70 euros per person, with tours lasting around three hours. These excursions respect distance rules and limit the number of boats allowed near the pods, ensuring wildlife remains undisturbed. Many companies also offer educational talks before departure, highlighting conservation efforts around the island.

Kayaking and paddle boarding in the calm lagoons of L'Hermitage and La Saline are low impact activities that allow visitors to explore without disturbing the fragile reef. Rentals are easy to find near the beaches, usually costing 10 to 15 euros per hour. Most rental stands open at 9.00 in the morning and close around 5.00 in the afternoon. Equipment is lightweight, and the lagoon's shallow waters make these activities safe even for beginners.

To further minimize environmental impact, travelers are encouraged to carry reusable water bottles, avoid single use plastics, and support locally owned accommodations and restaurants. Guesthouses in Salazie and Mafate often use solar power and source food directly from nearby farms, providing a sustainable alternative to larger resorts. Rates start around 40 euros per night including breakfast, and reservations can be made directly with the owners.

Exploring Réunion with care for the environment not only protects its unique ecosystems but also creates more authentic experiences. Walking through mountain villages, cycling between towns, or paddling quietly over the lagoon lets travelers connect more closely with the island while ensuring it remains unspoiled for future visitors.

Chapter 3

Understanding Réunion Island

A Short History of the Island

Réunion Island's history is shaped by waves of settlement, trade, and cultural blending that together formed the identity it carries today. For centuries the island remained uninhabited, known only to Arab sailors and navigators from Madagascar who passed through the Indian Ocean. It entered European records in the early sixteenth century when Portuguese explorers noted its presence, though they did not establish a settlement. The French East India Company claimed it in the seventeenth century, renaming it Île Bourbon, and soon after the first permanent settlers arrived from France, Madagascar, and Africa.

The early colony was small and depended heavily on supplies from passing ships. Over time, French settlers established coffee and later sugarcane plantations, which became the backbone of the economy. This system relied on enslaved labor, bringing people from Africa, Madagascar, and India to work under harsh conditions. The population grew diverse, but society remained marked by inequality. In 1848, France abolished slavery, and the island entered a new chapter. Freed men and women began building communities, while indentured workers from India and China arrived to fill labor shortages. These groups brought with them traditions, religions, and culinary practices that remain central to the island's character.

In the nineteenth and early twentieth centuries, sugarcane dominated the economy, and mills spread across the fertile plains. Exports tied the island closely to France, and despite its distance from Europe, French influence deepened. By the mid twentieth century, the island faced economic challenges, leading to migration programs that sent many young people to mainland France for work. In 1946, Réunion's political status shifted when it became a French overseas department, granting its residents full French citizenship and tying its administration, law, and education system directly to Paris.

The later twentieth century brought rapid modernization. Roads, hospitals, and schools expanded, linking mountain villages more closely to coastal towns. Tourism began to grow as travelers sought out its volcanic landscapes, beaches, and cultural mix. Today the island is not only a French department but also part of the European Union, using the euro and maintaining direct connections with Paris and other global hubs.

Travelers interested in learning more about this past can visit several sites. The Musée de Villèle in Saint Gilles offers insight into plantation life, with restored buildings set on an estate once run with enslaved labor. Entry costs around 6 euros, and it opens Tuesday to Sunday from 9.30 in the morning until 5.30 in the evening. In Saint Denis, the Léon Dierx Museum focuses on art but also preserves archives that trace colonial and cultural history. Smaller heritage centers in Salazie and Cilaos present exhibitions on rural life, mountain traditions, and the role of indentured workers.

What makes Réunion's history stand out is the way it created a society where African, European, Indian, Chinese, and Malagasy influences meet in daily life. Religion, music, food, and language carry traces of each origin, making the island a living record of centuries of encounters. This blend, born out of hardship and resilience, remains one of the strongest reasons visitors find the island so distinctive today.

Languages and Communication Essentials

French is the official language of Réunion Island and is used in schools, government offices, and the media. Travelers will find road signs, menus, and official documents written in French, so a basic understanding of the language is helpful. English is spoken in some hotels, resorts, and tour companies, but outside of these settings it is less common. Staff in larger restaurants and car rental agencies may understand it, though conversations are usually easier with French. Carrying a phrasebook or a translation app can make daily interactions smoother, particularly in markets and small towns where locals may not speak foreign languages.

Alongside French, Réunion Creole is widely spoken in daily life. It is the mother tongue for many residents and is used in music, storytelling, and informal conversations. While visitors are not expected to speak Creole, learning a few phrases such as bonzour for good morning or mersi for thank you often earns a warm response. Creole is a living reflection of the island's history, blending French vocabulary with words from Malagasy, Tamil, and African languages, and hearing it in markets or on buses adds to the cultural experience.

In hotels and airports, most staff communicate comfortably in French and some English, but in rural guesthouses or family run gîtes, French or Creole is essential. Tour guides usually speak several languages, with English, German, or Italian often available on request. Prices for guided tours in multiple languages are generally the same as standard rates, starting from around 40 euros for half day excursions. Tours can be arranged in Saint Gilles, Saint Denis, or Saint Pierre, where agencies open from 9.00 in the morning to 6.00 in the evening.

Telecommunication services are modern and reliable. Local SIM cards are sold at shops such as Orange, SFR, and Free in Saint Denis and major towns, with prices beginning at 10 euros for prepaid packages including calls, texts, and data. Shops usually open from Monday to Saturday between 9.00 in the morning and 6.00 in the evening. Mobile coverage is strong along the coast and in most towns, though signals may weaken in deep mountain valleys. Internet cafés are less common today as hotels and guesthouses provide Wi Fi, though connection speeds vary outside the main towns.

For simple tasks like ordering food or asking directions, visitors who make the effort to greet in French find that conversations flow more easily. Even short phrases such as bonsoir in the evening or s'il vous plaît when making a request add to the interaction. Locals are patient with travelers who try, and a polite approach is always appreciated. By combining a few French expressions with the island's relaxed pace, communication becomes part of the charm of traveling in Réunion.

Religion and Traditions in Everyday Life

Religion and traditions are woven into daily life in Réunion Island, shaping festivals, family gatherings, and even the rhythm of work and rest. Catholicism is the most widely practiced faith, a legacy of French colonization, and churches can be found in every town and village. Sunday services are well attended, with many families dressing formally and gathering afterwards for shared meals. In

Saint Denis, the Cathedral of Saint Denis stands as one of the most significant religious landmarks, opening daily from morning until evening with free entry for visitors.

Alongside Catholicism, Hinduism has a strong presence, brought by Indian workers who arrived in the nineteenth century. Temples across the island, particularly in Saint André and Saint Louis, display bright colors and intricate carvings. Visitors are welcome, though respectful dress and behavior are expected. During festivals such as Cavadee in January or February, processions fill the streets with music, flowers, and offerings. Participation is free, and watching these celebrations provides insight into the cultural depth of the island.

Islam also has a role in local life, with mosques in towns such as Saint Denis and Saint Pierre serving the Muslim community. Friday prayers draw large gatherings, and during Ramadan, markets and restaurants in certain neighborhoods take on a special atmosphere in the evenings. Chinese traditions, introduced by migrants from Canton and Hakka regions, are visible in temples like the Guan Di Temple in Saint Denis, which opens daily for worship and cultural events.

These religions coexist with ease, creating a sense of harmony unique to Réunion. It is common to see Catholic processions, Hindu ceremonies, and Chinese New Year festivities celebrated within the same year, each respected and embraced by the wider community. Traditional music and dance also reflect this blend. Sega and maloya, the island's two most important music styles, were born out of the history of slavery and resistance, carrying strong cultural meaning. Maloya, once banned because of its association with political expression, is now recognized by UNESCO as part of the world's intangible heritage. Performances can be seen in cultural centers or during festivals, often costing around 10 to 20 euros for an evening event.

Family traditions are just as important. Meals often bring several generations together, with dishes such as cari or rougail served alongside rice, beans, and fresh fruit. Respect for elders and strong family ties remain central to daily life. Even in busy towns, visitors will notice how much emphasis is placed on hospitality, with locals proud to share their culture with others.

Markets are another place where traditions are alive. Stalls selling flowers for offerings at temples stand next to vendors of Catholic rosaries or stalls with incense and candles. Prices are modest, with flowers starting at a few euros per bundle. These markets usually open early, around 6.00 in the morning, and continue until midday, closing when the heat becomes stronger.

In every part of the island, traditions are not limited to religious practices but extend to the way people live, celebrate, and share their heritage. Travelers who approach with respect and openness will find that attending a mass, visiting a temple, or listening to maloya are experiences that bring them closer to understanding the island's heart.

Festivals and Annual Celebrations

Festivals and celebrations in Réunion Island reflect the blend of cultures that shape the island's identity. The calendar is filled with religious events, music gatherings, and public holidays that bring communities together, often spilling into the streets with color, rhythm, and food.

In January or February, the Tamil festival of Cavadee is one of the most striking events. Centered in Saint André, it features long processions where devotees carry decorated wooden arches covered with flowers and offerings. Drumming and chanting set the atmosphere, and the devotion displayed during rituals leaves a strong impression on anyone watching. Visitors can attend freely, though modest clothing and respect for the ceremony are important. Shops and restaurants in Saint André often stay open late during this period, adding to the festive mood.

Catholic traditions remain equally strong, with processions during Easter and All Saints' Day observed across the island. During All Saints' Day on November 1, cemeteries glow with thousands of candles placed on graves by families. It is a time of remembrance but also of community, as families gather to share food and stories.

Chinese New Year is celebrated each year in Saint Denis, particularly around the Guan Di Temple. The streets fill with red lanterns, lion dances, and firecrackers, with food stalls serving dumplings and noodles alongside Creole specialties. The celebrations last several days, usually free to attend, with performances in the evenings.

Maloya and sega, the two iconic music styles of the island, take center stage during cultural festivals. The Festival Liberté Métisse in Saint Paul each December commemorates the abolition of slavery with concerts, dance, and theatre. Admission is free, and the event usually takes place on the beach, making it one of the most popular gatherings of the year. Another important event is Sakifo Musik Festival in Saint Pierre, held in June. It draws local and international artists across genres, with ticket prices starting from around 40 euros for a single day pass. Concerts are staged outdoors, often lasting until late at night, creating a lively atmosphere that attracts thousands.

Hindu festivals also mark the calendar with Diwali, known locally as Dipavali, celebrated in October or November. Towns light up with candles, oil lamps, and fireworks, while families prepare sweet dishes to share with neighbors. In Saint André and Saint Denis, cultural associations organize parades and shows, usually free, bringing together crowds of all backgrounds.

National events such as Bastille Day on July 14 are also celebrated, with military parades in Saint Denis and fireworks along the coast. Locals gather at beaches in the evening, enjoying food stalls and music until late.

Throughout the year, smaller festivals highlight food, film, and crafts, showcasing the creativity of the island. Village fairs in the cirques celebrate seasonal harvests with music and traditional dishes, often costing only a few euros for entry or food. Markets open early, usually from 6.00 in the morning, and continue until midday, adding a festive energy even outside major holidays.

The diversity of Réunion's celebrations means that no matter when you visit, there is likely to be a festival taking place. Each event is an invitation to see how communities honor their history, faith, and culture, turning ordinary days into unforgettable experiences filled with rhythm, flavor, and color.

Arts, Music, and Local Crafts

Arts, music, and crafts in Réunion Island reflect the mix of cultures that have shaped the island for centuries. Creole traditions, African rhythms, Indian influences, and French heritage all merge into expressions that feel both local and universal. Visitors will notice this creativity everywhere, from music echoing in village squares to handcrafted baskets and pottery displayed in markets.

Music is one of the strongest cultural markers. Sega and maloya are the two main traditional styles, both deeply tied to the island's history. Sega carries lively rhythms often accompanied by guitars, drums, and accordions, usually played at family gatherings and festivals. Maloya, once performed by enslaved communities, uses percussion instruments like the roulèr drum and kayamb, a flat instrument filled with seeds that creates a distinctive rattling sound. This music was banned for decades because of its political meaning, but today it is celebrated openly and is listed as UNESCO cultural heritage. Performances can be found in cultural centers such as Le Séchoir in Saint Leu, which hosts concerts and theatre. Tickets range from 10 to 25 euros depending on the event, with doors opening in the evening around 7.00.

Visual arts also have a strong presence. The Léon Dierx Museum in Saint Denis, located on Rue de Paris, presents collections ranging from European paintings to local creations. It opens Tuesday to Sunday from 9.30 in the morning until 5.30 in the evening, with entry priced at 5 euros. Smaller galleries and artist studios are scattered across the island, often run by local painters and sculptors who welcome visitors to see their work. These spaces usually open in the afternoons, and while entrance is free, many sell affordable pieces such as paintings or sculptures that capture scenes of island life.

Crafts are part of daily markets and village fairs. Basket weaving, pottery, and embroidery remain popular, with items created using natural materials such as vacoa leaves or bamboo. At the Saint Paul market, which takes place every Friday and Saturday near the seafront, visitors can buy handmade hats, woven bags, and wooden carvings. Prices start at around 10 euros, and the market is open from 6.00 in the morning until 1.00 in the afternoon. These items make meaningful souvenirs, as each piece reflects local traditions passed down through generations.

Dance is another cultural expression worth experiencing. Sega dancing is cheerful and accompanied by quick hip movements, often performed during festivals and family gatherings. Maloya dance is slower and more grounded, echoing the rhythm of drums. Cultural associations across towns such as Saint Denis and Saint Pierre organize performances, many free to watch during celebrations.

Street art has grown in recent years, especially in Saint Denis and Le Port, where murals cover walls with bold colors and themes ranging from local history to environmental awareness. Guided street art walks are offered in Saint Denis, costing about 15 euros per person and lasting two hours. These tours usually start in the late afternoon, allowing visitors to enjoy both the art and the lively atmosphere of the city.

For travelers seeking authentic cultural experiences, attending a music performance, buying crafts directly from artisans, or visiting local galleries provides an understanding of how Réunion's creativity is deeply connected to its history. Each song, carving, or woven basket tells a story of resilience and blending, giving visitors not just a souvenir but a piece of the island's living culture.

Chapter 4

Laws, Safety, and Visitor Rights

Local Laws Every Visitor Should Know

As a French overseas department, Réunion follows the same legal framework as mainland France, which means visitors are subject to French and European Union regulations. Carrying a valid identity card for European travelers or a passport for non European travelers is required at all times, as police can request identification during checks. Tourists from outside the European Union should also ensure they respect visa conditions, since overstaying can lead to fines or bans from future entry.

Driving laws are strictly enforced, with speed limits clearly marked and monitored by radar. The standard limit is 50 km per hour in towns, 80 km per hour on main roads, and up to 110 km per hour on dual carriageways. Fines for speeding are expensive and can be charged on the spot if police issue a ticket. Seat belts are compulsory for all passengers, and children under ten must be placed in approved car seats. The legal alcohol limit for drivers is 0.5 grams per liter of blood, lower than in some countries, and random checks are frequent, particularly during weekends and evenings. Refusing a breath test or exceeding the limit carries severe penalties, including heavy fines and the possibility of losing the right to drive in France.

Drug laws are also strict. Possession or use of illegal substances, even in small amounts, can lead to arrest and fines. Smoking is prohibited in enclosed public places such as restaurants, bars, and buses, with penalties applied for violations. Many establishments provide outdoor smoking areas, but it is always safer to ask before lighting a cigarette.

The island places strong emphasis on environmental protection. Hiking trails, marine reserves, and national parks have rules designed to preserve biodiversity. Picking plants, disturbing wildlife, or leaving rubbish behind is prohibited, with fines of up to 150 euros for violations. Fires are not allowed in protected areas, and camping outside designated sites requires permission. Fishing and collecting shells in certain lagoons are also restricted, with clear signs marking no fishing zones. Visitors planning outdoor activities should respect these rules, as they safeguard fragile ecosystems and are taken seriously by local authorities.

Beach safety rules are another important aspect. Swimming is only permitted in designated lagoon areas or in zones monitored by lifeguards. Shark risks are present along the open coast, and authorities strictly ban swimming or surfing in unmonitored areas. Breaking these rules not only risks personal safety but can also result in fines. Lifeguard posts are found in Saint Gilles and Saint Leu, usually staffed daily from 9.00 in the morning until 5.00 in the evening.

Alcohol consumption is restricted in public spaces. Drinking on beaches, parks, or streets is generally not allowed unless at organized events. Most bars and restaurants close around midnight, though in larger towns such as Saint Denis and Saint Pierre, nightclubs stay open later. Noise restrictions are enforced after 10.00 in the evening in residential areas, so travelers staying in guesthouses should keep gatherings quiet at night.

Respect for religious and cultural practices is also expected. Temples, churches, and mosques welcome visitors, but modest dress is required, and photography may be limited during ceremonies. Markets sell offerings such as flowers and candles for religious rituals, and prices are affordable, starting at a few euros. Purchasing these items helps support traditions while showing respect for the culture.

By keeping these laws in mind, travelers will avoid unnecessary problems and move easily through the island. Carrying identification, respecting road rules, observing environmental guidelines, and being mindful of local customs ensures that the visit remains pleasant and trouble free.

Safety Tips in Cities, Villages, and Remote Areas

Staying safe in Réunion Island requires a little awareness, as conditions vary between the cities, villages, and the remote interior. In urban areas such as Saint Denis or Saint Pierre, normal precautions are enough. Petty theft can occur, especially in busy markets or during festivals, so keeping wallets, phones, and cameras secure is sensible. Avoid leaving valuables in parked cars, particularly near beaches or hiking trailheads, as break ins occasionally happen. Banks in Saint Denis and other large towns operate from Monday to Friday between 8.30 in the morning and 4.00 in the afternoon, and ATMs are safe to use during daylight hours. At night, stick to well lit streets and avoid carrying large sums of cash.

In smaller villages and coastal towns, safety concerns are minimal, and hospitality is part of everyday life. Visitors walking through markets or staying in family run guesthouses will find a relaxed atmosphere, but it is still wise to respect local customs. Modest dress is appreciated when visiting temples and churches, and care should be taken not to trespass on private farmland. Most village shops and markets close by early evening, leaving the streets quiet at night.

The remote areas of the island, particularly the cirques of Mafate, Salazie, and Cilaos, demand more preparation. Mafate is only accessible on foot or by helicopter, so visitors should be physically prepared for long walks and bring adequate water, food, and basic supplies. Hiking paths are well marked, but weather can change suddenly, with fog or heavy rain reducing visibility. Starting early in the morning is best, as afternoons often bring clouds. Local mountain lodges, known as gîtes, provide safe accommodation for around 20 to 40 euros per night, including dinner, and bookings can be made in advance through offices in Saint Denis or Saint Paul. Always inform your host or guide of your route, as mobile reception is limited in the cirques.

Volcanic landscapes such as Piton de la Fournaise are spectacular but require caution. Trails cross rough terrain with little shelter, so good footwear, a hat, and sun protection are essential. Weather can shift quickly, and temperatures drop sharply in the evening. There are no entrance fees to the volcano, but guided tours starting from Bourg Murat cost about 50 to 80 euros per person and provide extra safety with experienced leaders who know the terrain.

The ocean is another area where safety matters. Shark incidents have been reported in past years, and authorities strictly enforce rules that ban swimming or surfing outside of designated lagoon zones or beaches with lifeguards. Always swim where signs indicate it is permitted, such as the beaches of L'Hermitage and La Saline, where natural coral reefs provide protection. Lifeguard posts are usually open daily from 9.00 in the morning until 5.00 in the evening. Strong currents can occur even within lagoons, so staying near monitored areas is best.

For medical emergencies, dial 15 for ambulance services. Hospitals in Saint Denis and Saint Pierre operate 24 hours a day, while rural clinics keep shorter hours, generally from 8.00 in the morning until 5.00 in the afternoon. Pharmacies in towns display green crosses and open Monday to Saturday, with one pharmacy in each area rotating overnight duty for emergencies.

By remaining aware in cities, showing respect in villages, and preparing carefully in remote regions, travelers can move confidently through Réunion Island. With thoughtful planning, the focus stays on the island's landscapes, culture, and warmth of its people rather than on preventable problems.

Rules for Hiking and Nature Conservation

Hiking in Réunion Island is one of the most rewarding ways to experience its landscapes, but the trails come with clear rules to ensure both safety and the protection of fragile ecosystems. The island's national park covers more than forty percent of its territory, including Piton de la Fournaise, the cirques, and much of the highland forest, and regulations here are strict. Trails are free to access and well marked, but walkers are expected to stay on designated paths. Straying from the marked routes not only increases the risk of accidents but also damages soil and plants that are slow to recover.

Fires and open cooking are forbidden in the park and on mountain trails. Portable stoves may be used in designated picnic spots, but outside these areas the risk of wildfires is too high. Camping is allowed only in authorized areas or in the gardens of gîtes, with fees usually starting at 5 to 10 euros per night for a tent pitch. Many hikers choose to stay in gîtes, which cost around 20 to 40 euros for a bed, with dinner and breakfast available at additional cost. These lodges, located in Salazie, Cilaos, and Mafate, are part of the island's hiking culture and offer safe and legal overnight stays.

Waste disposal is another important rule. Everything carried into the park must be taken out, as bins are rare on trails. Leaving litter, even small items like fruit peels, is fined by authorities, and rangers patrol popular routes to enforce these measures. Water sources in the mountains may not always be safe to drink, so carrying purification tablets or filters is advised. Bottled water is available in villages before starting longer hikes, costing about one euro for 1.5 liters in local shops.

Respect for wildlife is central to nature conservation. Feeding animals is not allowed, as it disrupts their natural behavior. Birds such as the papangue, an endemic harrier, and the tuit-tuit, one of the rarest songbirds, are sensitive to disturbance. Noise should be kept low, and photography should not interfere with their habitats. Collecting plants or flowers is also prohibited, as many species are endemic and protected. Signs throughout the national park remind visitors of these restrictions, with fines imposed for violations.

Weather conditions must also be considered part of responsible hiking. Trails in Mafate and Cilaos can flood quickly during heavy rain, and landslides are possible after storms. The park service posts updates at trailheads and online, but hikers should also check conditions with local offices in Saint Denis or Bourg Murat before setting out. Setting off early in the morning is recommended, as cloud and rain build by midday. Trails are usually open year round, but during cyclone warnings access may be closed for safety.

Guided hikes provide an extra layer of security and education. Certified mountain guides explain the geology, flora, and cultural history while ensuring visitors respect park regulations. Prices start around 50 euros for a half day and rise to 80 or 100 euros for a full day in areas such as Piton de la Fournaise. Guides can be booked in advance at agencies in Saint Denis, Saint Pierre, or through accommodations in mountain villages.

Nature conservation extends beyond the mountains to the island's coastline. The lagoon on the west coast is a marine reserve where fishing, spear hunting, and collecting coral are banned. Snorkeling is permitted, but touching or standing on coral is not. Lifeguards and rangers enforce these rules, and fines apply for violations. Kayak and paddleboard rentals in Saint Gilles and L'Hermitage usually cost 10 to 15 euros per hour, with operators providing instructions on how to protect the lagoon.

By respecting these rules, hikers and nature lovers help preserve Réunion's landscapes for future generations. Staying on marked trails, carrying waste out, observing wildlife without interference, and supporting local gîtes and guides are all part of traveling responsibly. The reward is access to some of the most striking volcanic scenery in the world, enjoyed in a way that keeps it as unspoiled as possible.

Emergency Services and Useful Numbers

In Réunion Island, emergency services operate with the same efficiency as in mainland France, and knowing the right numbers ensures quick assistance when needed. For medical emergencies, dialing 15 connects you directly to ambulance services, which are available around the clock. Hospitals in Saint Denis, Saint Pierre, and Saint Benoît provide full emergency care, with the University Hospital in Saint Denis being the largest facility. Emergency rooms remain open 24 hours a day, and consultations in public hospitals generally follow the French system where fees are regulated. A standard consultation with a doctor costs about 25 euros, though costs can be higher for specialists. Travelers without European health cards or local coverage must pay upfront, so having travel insurance with medical coverage is highly recommended.

For police assistance, the number to call is 17. The gendarmerie maintains stations across towns and villages, with the main office in Saint Denis located at Rue de Paris, open daily from 8.00 in the morning to 6.00 in the evening. These services respond to theft, accidents, and public safety issues, with patrols visible in both urban and rural areas.

In case of fire or rescue needs, particularly common in mountain areas or during floods, dialing 18 reaches the fire brigade. They also handle search and rescue operations in the cirques and on the volcano. Helicopter rescues are coordinated from Gillot near the airport and are often used for emergencies in Mafate or along steep hiking trails. These services are efficient but costly without insurance that covers evacuation.

A single European emergency number, 112, also works across the island, connecting to the appropriate service based on the situation.

This is useful for visitors who may not remember each specific number. Calls are free from mobile phones and public booths.

Pharmacies, marked by green crosses, provide advice for minor health concerns and can recommend nearby doctors. Most pharmacies open Monday to Saturday from 8.30 in the morning until 6.30 in the evening, closing for a couple of hours at midday. One pharmacy in each district rotates night duty, and the address is displayed on the doors of local shops and clinics.

Tourists should also note the number 196, dedicated to sea rescue, which is important for those planning water activities. Lifeguard stations along the west coast beaches, particularly in Saint Gilles and L'Hermitage, are open daily from 9.00 in the morning until 5.00 in the evening. These posts not only provide rescue services but also offer advice on safe swimming zones.

For embassy or consular support, travelers must rely on French embassies in their home countries before arrival, since Réunion hosts no foreign embassies. In the event of lost passports or legal issues, local police can issue a report, but replacement travel documents are processed through embassies in Paris or Mauritius.

By keeping these numbers at hand, travelers can move around with confidence. Whether in cities, villages, or remote hiking areas, emergency services on the island are professional and responsive, and a little preparation ensures that help is only a call away whenever it is needed.

Respectful Behavior and Cultural Etiquette

Showing respect in Réunion Island comes naturally when travelers pay attention to local customs and approach people with politeness. Greetings are important, and a simple bonjour in the morning or bonsoir in the evening goes a long way. In shops, markets, or restaurants, acknowledging the staff before asking for something is considered courteous. Handshakes are common in formal settings, while friends and family often exchange kisses on both cheeks. Visitors who attempt even a few words of French or Creole will notice warmer responses, as locals appreciate the effort.

When visiting religious sites such as Hindu temples, churches, or mosques, modest clothing is expected. Shoulders and knees should be covered, and hats removed before entering. Photography is usually allowed outside, but it is polite to ask before taking pictures during ceremonies. Many temples and churches remain open during the day, often from 9.00 in the morning to 5.00 in the afternoon, with entry free of charge. Donations are welcome and help maintain the sites.

In restaurants, patience is part of the dining experience. Meals are often enjoyed at a slower pace, especially in Creole households and smaller eateries. Tipping is not mandatory since service is included in the bill, but rounding up or leaving a euro or two for good service is appreciated. Sharing food is common at family tables, and travelers staying in guesthouses may be invited to join communal meals. Accepting such invitations with gratitude shows respect for the hospitality offered.

Markets are lively and filled with local produce, crafts, and spices. Bargaining is not a strong tradition, but polite negotiation may be possible for handicrafts. Always remain friendly, and a smile will usually bring better results than pushing too hard on price. Stalls often open around 6.00 in the morning and close by midday, so arriving early shows consideration for vendors who work long hours.

Respect for the environment is another part of etiquette. Littering is frowned upon, and fines apply in national parks and reserves. On beaches, leaving rubbish behind is considered disrespectful, not only to locals but also to the community that relies on tourism. Smoking is restricted in many public spaces, and checking for signs before lighting a cigarette is advised.

When taking part in cultural events or festivals, blending in with the rhythm of the occasion is best. Whether it is the Cavadee procession in Saint André or sega dancing at a village celebration, observing first and participating respectfully shows appreciation. Many performances are free, while others may charge small entry fees of around 10 to 20 euros, usually announced in advance.

Hospitality in Réunion is generous, but visitors are expected to be equally considerate. Removing shoes when entering a private home is common, and offering a small gift such as fruit or wine when invited for a meal is seen as thoughtful. Engaging in conversations about the island's culture and history is welcomed, but political or sensitive topics are better avoided unless raised by locals.

By following these simple practices, travelers will find that interactions on the island become more rewarding. Respect, politeness, and openness ensure that encounters with people and traditions feel genuine, allowing visitors to connect meaningfully with the island's community.

Chapter 5

Where to Stay

Luxury Resorts on the Coast

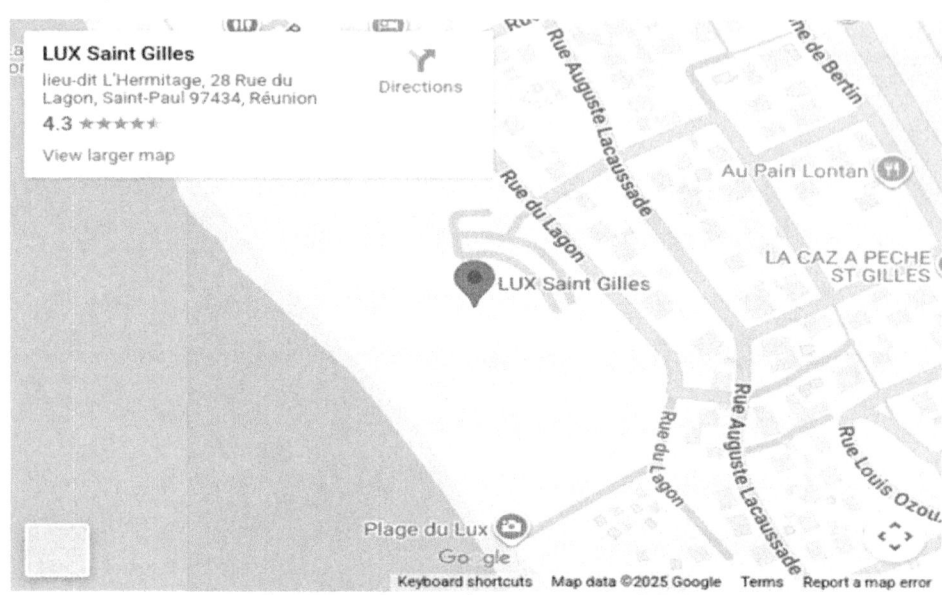

The coast of Réunion Island is home to a collection of luxury resorts that combine French sophistication with the relaxed spirit of the tropics. Most of these properties are found on the western shore around Saint Gilles and L'Hermitage, where the lagoon provides calm waters and long stretches of white sand. Staying here offers more than just comfort, as guests are treated to sunsets over the Indian Ocean and easy access to both marine activities and fine dining.

LUX* Saint Gilles is one of the most prestigious resorts on the island, located along L'Hermitage Beach. It offers spacious rooms set in colonial style villas surrounded by tropical gardens. The lagoon is just steps away, and the resort provides direct access to the beach with loungers reserved for guests. Facilities include a large swimming pool, tennis courts, and several restaurants serving both Creole and French cuisine. Prices start around 250 euros per night for a double room, with higher rates during peak season. The resort operates year round, with check in from 2.00 in the afternoon and check out at 11.00 in the morning.

Another highlight is Ness by D-Ocean, positioned at La Saline les Bains. This resort blends modern design with natural elements, offering suites with sea views and private terraces. A wellness center, infinity pool, and gourmet dining make it popular with couples seeking relaxation. Rooms begin at approximately 220 euros per night, with spa treatments available from 60 euros. The property is open daily, and the reception desk provides assistance for excursions such as paragliding, diving, or guided hikes.

For travelers seeking something more intimate, Hotel Blue Margouillat in Saint Leu combines boutique charm with luxury service. Perched above the sea, it has panoramic views, a fine dining restaurant specializing in French Creole fusion, and rooms decorated with original artworks. Nightly rates start at 300 euros, and the restaurant welcomes both guests and outside visitors, opening for lunch from 12.00 to 2.00 and for dinner from 7.00 to 9.30. Reservations are essential, especially on weekends.

Iloha Seaview Hotel near Saint Leu offers a slightly more relaxed luxury option, with bungalows and villas scattered across a hillside garden. Facilities include two swimming pools, a spa, and restaurants serving both international dishes and local specialties. Prices begin at 180 euros per night, making it one of the more accessible upscale stays. The resort is particularly well located for excursions to the mountains and marine reserve.

Resorts along the west coast often provide water sports equipment, fitness centers, and kids' clubs, making them suitable for both couples and families. Most properties also arrange airport transfers from Roland Garros, which takes about an hour by car. Shuttle services usually cost between 60 and 90 euros per trip, depending on distance.

Staying in a coastal resort ensures both comfort and convenience, with the lagoon offering safe swimming and snorkeling, while bars and restaurants nearby add nightlife and entertainment. The combination of attentive service, modern amenities, and natural surroundings makes these properties a strong choice for travelers who want to enjoy Réunion with a touch of luxury.

Budget-friendly Hotels and Guesthouses

Budget friendly hotels and guesthouses in Réunion Island provide comfort without unnecessary expense, making them ideal for travelers who want to enjoy the island while keeping costs under control. Many of these properties are family run, offering a warm welcome and a more personal experience than larger resorts. Rooms are simple but clean, often with terraces or garden views, and breakfasts featuring fresh bread, fruit, and local jams are usually included in the price.

In Saint Denis, small hotels near Rue de Paris and around the city center offer convenient stays for those arriving or departing from Roland Garros Airport. Nightly rates begin at around 60 euros for a double room, with check in typically from 2.00 in the afternoon and check out by 11.00 in the morning. These hotels usually provide free Wi Fi and easy access to restaurants and shops, though parking can be limited in the city.

On the west coast, guesthouses in Saint Gilles and La Saline les Bains place travelers close to the lagoon without the expense of luxury resorts. Rooms in these properties generally cost between 70 and 100 euros per night, with options ranging from small studios with kitchenettes to rooms in traditional Creole houses. Many guesthouses are located within walking distance of beaches, and some owners offer bicycles for rent at modest prices. Shops and beachside restaurants open daily from morning until late evening, making it easy to enjoy local food without traveling far.

The cirques of Salazie and Cilaos are also well known for affordable gîtes and mountain guesthouses. These provide shared meals, dormitory style rooms, and private doubles, with prices starting around 20 euros for a bed in a dorm and 50 euros for a private room with half board. Meals are often communal, with hearty dishes like chicken cari and lentils served at long tables, creating an atmosphere that encourages conversation among hikers. Most gîtes open year round, though advance booking is recommended in peak season, especially in Cilaos where accommodation fills quickly on weekends.

In coastal towns such as Saint Pierre, budget hotels close to the waterfront offer easy access to nightlife and markets. Prices range from 70 to 90 euros per night, with many rooms featuring balconies or sea views at a fraction of the cost of nearby resorts. Guesthouses in this area often have shared kitchens, which helps travelers reduce costs by cooking their own meals with produce bought from the local market.

For travelers who want more independence, apartments and small holiday rentals are widely available. These often cost between 50 and 80 euros per night and include basic cooking facilities. Supermarkets in Saint Denis, Saint Gilles, and Saint Pierre open daily from 8.00 in the morning until 8.00 in the evening, making it easy to shop for supplies.

Budget accommodation in Réunion may not offer the luxury of resorts, but the personal touch, convenient locations, and affordable prices make them attractive options. Whether it is a gîte in the mountains, a Creole style guesthouse by the lagoon, or a small hotel in the city, these stays provide everything needed for a comfortable base while leaving more of the budget available for exploring the island's landscapes, food, and cultural experiences.

Charming Bed and Breakfasts

Charming bed and breakfasts in Réunion Island bring travelers closer to the heart of local life, offering hospitality that feels personal and authentic. Many are run by Creole families who open their homes to visitors, sharing not only a comfortable room but also stories, recipes, and traditions passed down through generations. These stays are scattered across the island, from the lively towns on the coast to the tranquil villages in the mountains, giving guests a choice between ocean views and green valleys.

Along the west coast near Saint Gilles and La Saline, bed and breakfasts often sit within walking distance of the lagoon. Rooms are usually decorated in Creole style with wooden furniture, bright textiles, and shaded verandas where breakfast is served. Rates range from 70 to 100 euros per night for two people, with breakfast of fresh bread, pastries, local fruit, and coffee included. Hosts often provide advice on nearby beaches, restaurants, and water activities, helping guests discover spots beyond the typical tourist trail.

In the mountain regions, particularly around Salazie and Cilaos, bed and breakfasts offer cozy stays surrounded by dramatic peaks and waterfalls. Wooden chalets and Creole houses with flower filled gardens provide simple yet warm accommodation, perfect after a day of hiking. Nightly rates begin at 60 euros for a double room with breakfast, while some properties also serve homemade dinners for an additional 15 to 20 euros per person. These meals often feature cari, lentils, and seasonal fruit, enjoyed around a family table. Staying in such places adds a sense of belonging, as guests share meals with hosts and other travelers.

Saint Pierre, known for its lively market and waterfront, also has several small bed and breakfasts tucked into quiet streets near the center. Prices here average 80 to 110 euros per night, with many properties offering terraces or small courtyards shaded by bougainvillea. From these locations, it is easy to explore the market in the morning, enjoy the town's nightlife, and return to a restful setting by evening.

Some of the most memorable stays are found in the cirques, especially Mafate, which can only be reached on foot. Here, small family run lodgings provide rustic comfort to hikers. Rooms are simple, with shared facilities, but the hospitality makes up for the lack of luxury. A night in Mafate usually costs about 40 euros with breakfast and dinner included. Since supplies are carried in by mule or helicopter, meals are based on local produce and often served communally, adding to the sense of connection between travelers and hosts.

Bed and breakfasts across the island typically welcome guests in the afternoon from 2.00 onwards, with check out by 11.00 the next morning. Reservations can be made directly online or through tourist offices in towns such as Saint Denis and Saint Gilles. These accommodations are particularly popular during holidays, so advance booking is advised.

Choosing a bed and breakfast in Réunion not only provides affordable comfort but also creates lasting encounters with the people of the island. The chance to enjoy home cooked meals, learn a few Creole words, and share in local rhythms makes these stays an enriching part of any journey. They may not have the scale of resorts, but what they offer in warmth and cultural experience often leaves the strongest impression.

Mountain Lodges and Gîtes in the Cirques

Mountain lodges and gîtes in the cirques of Réunion Island are an essential part of the hiking experience, offering a warm welcome after a long day on the trails. Scattered across Salazie, Cilaos, and Mafate, these accommodations are simple but full of character, blending comfort with local hospitality. They allow travelers to rest, enjoy hearty meals, and connect with the communities that live in these remote mountain settings.

In Cilaos, gîtes are plentiful, ranging from family run guesthouses to larger lodges with dormitories and private rooms. Prices start at around 20 euros for a dorm bed and 50 euros for a double room, often including breakfast. Dinner is usually served communally, with dishes like lentils grown on the slopes of Cilaos, chicken cari, and seasonal fruit. Meals typically cost 15 to 20 euros per person and are shared at large tables, where conversation between hikers adds to the atmosphere. Cilaos can be reached by road, with the winding route of over 400 bends leading up from Saint Louis, so supplies are easier to transport and facilities are slightly more developed.

Salazie offers another range of gîtes, often in Creole style houses surrounded by gardens and waterfalls. Staying here costs about the same as in Cilaos, with rooms between 50 and 70 euros including breakfast. Dinner is home cooked and hearty, designed to refuel hikers after a day on the trails. Villages such as Hell Bourg are known for their charm, and many lodges here also offer cultural activities such as cooking lessons or garden visits. Most properties open year round, welcoming hikers from early afternoon until evening. Check in is normally from 2.00, with check out before 11.00 the next day.

Mafate is unique, as it has no road access and can only be reached on foot or by helicopter. This isolation gives its gîtes a rustic feel, but also a sense of reward for those who make the journey. Beds cost about 40 euros per night with breakfast and dinner included, reflecting the effort of transporting supplies by mule or helicopter. Rooms are simple, sometimes shared, and facilities may be basic, but the hospitality of the hosts makes every stay memorable. The meals are usually rich stews or curries, served with rice and lentils, prepared with whatever is available locally. Booking ahead is recommended, particularly on weekends and holidays when hikers fill the limited number of rooms. Reservations can be made through tourist offices or directly with the lodge owners.

Electricity in mountain gîtes is sometimes limited, with solar panels or generators providing power. Guests should not expect strong internet connections, as mobile coverage is weak in the cirques, particularly Mafate. This lack of connectivity is part of the appeal, encouraging visitors to disconnect and enjoy the stillness of the mountains. Hot water is available in most lodges, though in Mafate it can be inconsistent.

Many gîtes provide packed lunches for an additional cost of around 8 to 10 euros, convenient for hikers continuing their journey the next morning. Payment is usually in cash, as card facilities are rare in remote areas. Shops in Saint Paul, Saint Pierre, or Saint Denis should be used to withdraw money before heading into the mountains.

Staying in a gîte is more than just finding a bed; it is part of the rhythm of hiking in Réunion. The shared meals, early mornings, and conversations with fellow walkers create a sense of community that adds depth to the journey. From the accessibility of Cilaos to the remoteness of Mafate, mountain lodges are where travelers experience the island's heart most closely, surrounded by peaks, forests, and the hospitality of people who call these extraordinary landscapes home.

Unique Stays

Unique stays in Réunion Island are designed for travelers looking for more than a bed for the night, offering a chance to experience the island's landscapes and traditions in an unforgettable way. Treehouses, eco lodges, Creole villas, and luxury tents are spread across different corners of the island, each with its own character and appeal. These places mix comfort with creativity, blending natural surroundings with thoughtful design and a sense of adventure.

Treehouses are especially popular in the highland areas around Plaine des Palmistes and Entre Deux. Perched above the ground, they offer sweeping views of forests and valleys, often with balconies that look out over the lush greenery. Prices usually range from 120 to 180 euros per night for two people, with breakfast included. Many of these stays offer homemade jams, fresh bread, and tropical fruit in the morning. Check in is usually from 3.00 and check out before 11.00. These properties tend to be small, often with just a handful of cabins, so booking early is essential.

Eco lodges in places like Sainte Suzanne or near Cirque de Salazie focus on sustainability while still offering a high standard of comfort. They use solar panels for energy and collect rainwater for showers. The interiors are often simple but elegant, with natural materials and open spaces that connect directly to gardens or forests. Prices range from 100 to 150 euros per night depending on the level of service. Some eco lodges also provide guided activities such as waterfall walks or yoga sessions, usually at an additional fee of 20 to 30 euros per person.

Creole villas are another distinctive option, particularly in the coastal towns of Saint Gilles les Bains and Saint Pierre. Many of these homes are over a century old, renovated with care to keep their original charm. Wooden verandas, colorful shutters, and lush gardens make them an atmospheric choice for visitors who want to feel part of local life. A stay in such a villa costs between 90 and 140 euros per night, depending on the size and location. Some are self catering, while others offer breakfast or even a private chef for an extra charge.

For travelers who prefer a closer connection to nature, luxury tents and lodges set in the wild landscapes of the island provide a different kind of escape. Locations near Grand Étang or the volcano areas are particularly striking, with tents offering proper beds, private bathrooms, and even hot tubs under the stars. Prices can vary from 130 to 200 euros per night, with many sites including breakfast and dinner prepared with local produce. These stays are popular with couples looking for a romantic setting as well as adventurers who want comfort without losing the feel of the outdoors.

Some farms in the highlands also open their doors to visitors, giving guests the chance to stay in working agricultural settings. Known as table d'hôtes, these stays usually cost around 70 to 100 euros per night including meals. Guests often share rustic dining tables with the host family, eating dishes made from produce grown on the farm itself. The experience is simple yet authentic, and many travelers find it to be a highlight of their time on the island.

Each unique stay comes with its own rhythm and charm. Whether it is waking up in a treehouse to the sound of birds, stepping out of a villa into a lively coastal town, or watching stars from a tent in the highlands, these options turn a night's rest into part of the journey. They not only provide a place to sleep but also allow travelers to connect with the landscapes and people of Réunion in ways that standard hotels cannot match.

Chapter 6

Food and Culinary Experiences

Traditional Creole Cuisine Explained

Traditional Creole cuisine in Réunion Island is a story of cultures that came together over centuries, mixing French, African, Indian and Chinese influences into dishes that are full of flavor and character. At its heart is the cari, a dish that travelers will see on almost every menu. Cari is usually prepared with chicken, fish, or seafood, simmered with turmeric, onions, garlic, ginger and tomatoes, and always served with rice. It is the island's comfort food, eaten in homes, small roadside eateries and high end restaurants alike. A typical plate costs between 8 and 15 euros in local canteens, and from 18 to 25 euros in more refined establishments.

Alongside cari, another staple is rougail, which can mean two things. There is rougail as a main dish, usually made with sausage, pork, or salted fish in a tomato based sauce, and rougail as a condiment, which is a fiery mix of chilies, ginger, and herbs often served in small bowls to add heat to the meal. The condiment is free with most meals, while a full rougail dish costs about 12 to 20 euros depending on where it is ordered. The use of spice is central to the food culture here, and restaurants will usually ask how much heat a guest can handle before serving.

Street food plays a big role in understanding Creole cooking. Snacks known as bouchons, which are steamed dumplings filled with pork or chicken, are sold in small packets for around 2 to 3 euros in bakeries or street stalls. Samoussas, another popular bite, come with fillings like meat, cheese or vegetables and cost about 1 euro each. They are eaten throughout the day and are often washed down with a Dodo, the local beer named after the bird that once roamed nearby islands.

Sweet treats highlight another side of Creole tradition. Bonbons piment, which despite the name are savory fritters made with split peas and chili, are found in markets and fairs. For desserts, visitors often try gateau patate, a cake made from sweet potatoes, vanilla and sugar, or tropical fruit tarts showcasing mango, pineapple and lychee. Prices for pastries in bakeries usually range from 2 to 4 euros.

Creole cuisine is also inseparable from the ritual of dining together. On weekends, families gather for long meals that can last most of the afternoon, starting with an aperitif of rhum arrangé. This local rum is flavored with fruit, spices, or coffee beans, and served in small glasses before the main meal. Many restaurants, particularly in Saint Denis and Saint Pierre, offer tastings of rhum arrangé for around 5 to 8 euros per glass.

For travelers interested in learning more, several cooking schools in towns such as Saint Gilles and Hell Bourg run workshops where guests prepare traditional dishes under the guidance of Creole chefs. A half day class, usually starting around 9.00 and finishing by 14.00, costs between 50 and 70 euros and often includes lunch with the dishes prepared.

Markets are another place where food and culture come together. The Saturday market at Saint Paul, running from early morning until around 14.00, is one of the best known, with rows of stalls selling spices, fresh produce, chutneys and sweets. A bag of mixed local spices costs about 5 to 7 euros and makes a meaningful souvenir as well as a way to recreate the flavors at home.

Eating in Réunion is not just about satisfying hunger but about experiencing how history, culture and nature shaped the island. From the rich sauces of cari to the spice filled bites from street stalls, every dish carries a piece of the island's story, making the food as much a reason to visit as the landscapes themselves.

Street Food and Local Snacks to Try

Street food in Réunion Island is more than a quick bite, it is an expression of the island's mixed heritage and a gateway into daily life. The best way to taste it is to visit markets, small stalls along the roads, or bakeries that stock savory snacks throughout the day. Prices are low, usually between one and three euros, which makes it easy to try several specialties in one sitting without stretching the budget.

Samoussas are among the most familiar, triangular pockets filled with spiced meat, tuna, cheese or vegetables, fried until crisp and golden. They are sold everywhere from market stalls in Saint Paul to corner bakeries in Saint Denis, often for just one euro each. Locals often buy them by the dozen for gatherings, so do not be surprised to see long queues in front of vendors by midday.

Bouchons are another favorite. These small dumplings, inspired by Chinese cuisine but adapted to local tastes, are usually stuffed with pork, chicken or shrimp. They are steamed and served in small paper cones with soy sauce or chili. In towns like Saint Pierre, food trucks set up in the evening around 18.00 and sell bouchons for about two to three euros for a portion of five pieces. Many travelers pair them with a bottle of Dodo, the island's famous beer, sold for around three euros at the same stands.

Sweet and savory fritters known as bonbons piment are found in most markets. Despite their name, they are not sugary treats but crunchy bites made from ground split peas mixed with chili and coriander, shaped into small balls and fried. A small bag usually costs two to three euros and is perfect as a snack while walking through the busy aisles of Saint Paul's Saturday market, which runs from 7.00 to 14.00 near the seafront.

Other tempting choices include beignets, which can be sweet or salty. Banana beignets are popular for breakfast or dessert and usually sold for one to two euros each. Fish beignets, seasoned with turmeric and garlic, are slightly heavier and often eaten with rougail sauce on the side. Both are staples at stalls in smaller towns and villages, often appearing in the late afternoon when locals stop by for a quick bite before dinner.

One of the most distinctive snacks is the American sandwich, a hearty baguette stuffed with fries, meat, salad and sauce, sold in roadside food trucks across the island. Though not traditional in origin, it has become a local classic. Prices range from four to six euros, and the sandwiches are usually served until late at night, making them a favorite after long days at the beach or hikes in the mountains.

Travelers who want to taste a variety of snacks in one place should not miss the Saint Denis fairground on weekends, where dozens of vendors open from morning until evening. Here, samoussas, bouchons, fritters and grilled corn are sold side by side, allowing visitors to try everything in one go. It is also a place to hear sega music playing in the background while families share plates of snacks at communal tables.

Street food in Réunion Island is both affordable and deeply tied to its culture. Every bite tells a part of the story, whether it is a samoussa passed down from Indian migrants, a bouchon brought by Chinese settlers, or a fritter inspired by Creole traditions. Eating at the stalls and markets is not only about food, it is about being part of the island's rhythm, where flavors, sounds and people come together in a way that defines local life.

Fresh Market Finds: Fruits, Spices, and Coffee

Markets in Réunion Island are places where the scent of fresh fruit, roasting coffee and fragrant spices fills the air before you even step inside. The Saint Paul Market, held every Friday from 6.00 to 18.00 and Saturday from 6.00 to 14.00 along the waterfront, is one of the most popular and offers the widest selection. Here you will find stalls stacked with mangoes, pineapples, lychees in season, papayas and jackfruit, all grown in the island's fertile soil. Prices are reasonable, usually two to three euros per kilo for most fruit, and vendors often let you taste before buying.

Spices are another highlight. Turmeric, known locally as curcuma, is sold in powdered form or as fresh roots, giving a golden color and warm flavor to Creole dishes. Small packets of cloves, cinnamon sticks and nutmeg are sold from around one to three euros each, making them easy to take home as souvenirs. At some stalls you can watch women preparing massalé spice blends by hand, a mixture of coriander, cumin, fenugreek and mustard seeds that forms the backbone of many family recipes.

Coffee has deep roots on the island, especially in the highland region of Saint Leu and the Bras Panon area. The bourbon pointu variety, once nearly lost and now carefully cultivated again, is considered one of the finest in the world for its smoothness and floral notes. At the Saint Denis Market, which opens Tuesday to Sunday from 6.00 to 17.00 near Rue Maréchal Leclerc, vendors sell freshly roasted beans for about eight to ten euros per small bag. You will often be offered a cup to taste before deciding, and it is worth taking the time to talk with growers who are proud of their heritage.

Aside from the two main markets, smaller village markets such as Cilaos, open on Sundays from 7.00 to 13.00 in the town square, give a chance to shop directly from farmers. There you will see baskets of lentils from the mountain terraces, vanilla pods carefully wrapped in glass tubes, and jars of honey flavored by local flowers. Prices can vary depending on the rarity, with vanilla costing between two and five euros per pod depending on quality.

Visiting these markets is not just about shopping but about experiencing a way of life. Locals come early in the morning to chat with friends while filling their baskets, and the buzz of conversation mixes with the clatter of knives chopping sugarcane into sweet sticks for children. Vendors are usually happy to explain how to use spices or prepare fruit, so it feels like a lesson as much as a purchase. The colors, scents and flavors combine into a memorable part of any trip, and the goods you take away continue to tell the story long after leaving the island.

Fine Dining and French Influences

Dining in Réunion Island often feels like a journey between two worlds, where Creole warmth meets French refinement at the same table. The island has no shortage of casual eateries, but those looking for an elevated experience will find restaurants that blend Parisian elegance with local ingredients in surprising ways. In Saint Denis, establishments such as Le Roland Garros on Rue de Paris offer multi course menus that highlight freshly caught fish prepared with French sauces, paired with wines brought from Bordeaux and Burgundy. Expect to pay around forty to sixty euros for a three course meal, with service running daily from 12.00 to 14.00 for lunch and 19.00 to 22.00 for dinner.

Along the west coast in Saint Gilles, La Table du Boucan at LUX Saint Gilles resort is known for its intimate setting and creative approach. Lobster from local waters might be served with vanilla butter, while duck breast is glazed with mango and accompanied by root vegetables. Desserts often feature passionfruit, pineapple or the island's prized bourbon vanilla. Prices reflect the quality, with set menus ranging from sixty to ninety euros. Reservations are advised, especially during weekends and holiday periods, and the restaurant typically opens from 19.00 to 22.30.

French influences are also present in bistros that balance fine dining with a relaxed atmosphere. In Saint Pierre, Le Jardin de l'Orangeraie presents dishes such as foie gras terrine or beef tenderloin with red wine reduction, alongside Creole flavors like lentil ragout or palm heart salad. The menu changes with the season, and lunch service can be enjoyed from 12.00 to 14.00, with dinner from 19.00 to 22.00. Prices here average between thirty and fifty euros per person.

For travelers who enjoy exploring food with a view, the highland town of Cilaos has small gourmet restaurants where French tradition finds a rustic touch. At Le Vieux Cep Hotel's restaurant, trout from mountain streams is served with lemon butter, followed by a cheese course featuring imports from mainland France. Meals usually cost about thirty to forty euros, with service hours from 12.00 to 14.00 and 19.00 to 21.00. Dining in this mountain setting combines refinement with the quiet atmosphere of the cirque.

Wine and champagne play an important role in these experiences, and most fine dining restaurants keep carefully curated lists that favor French vineyards but also showcase South African and New World bottles. Paired tastings often add fifteen to twenty euros per person to the meal. Service is attentive and professional, maintaining the French tradition of hospitality, while still carrying the friendliness of island life. Dining this way in Réunion Island shows how French gastronomy has been embraced and reinterpreted, creating meals that remain memorable long after leaving the table.

Rum, Sugarcane, and Island Drinks

Rum is at the heart of Réunion Island's drinking culture, and its roots lie in the sugarcane fields that cover much of the landscape. Distilleries across the island produce agricole rum, made from freshly pressed cane juice rather than molasses, giving it a distinctive grassy and aromatic character. Many travelers head to Savanna Distillery in Saint André or Rivière du Mât near Saint Benoît, where tours walk visitors through the process from cane cutting to barrel aging. Most tours cost between eight and twelve euros, often including a guided tasting. Opening hours generally run from 9.00 to 17.00 on weekdays, with reduced hours on Saturday mornings.

One of the island's most beloved drinks is rhum arrangé, where local white rum is infused with fruits, spices, or vanilla pods. Every family and bar has its own recipe, and flavors can range from pineapple and lychee to cinnamon and ginger. A glass in a bar or seaside café usually costs between four and seven euros, and it is often served as an aperitif before a meal. Bottled versions can be purchased at markets in Saint Paul or Saint Pierre, where vendors happily explain their blends and offer small samples.

Sugarcane juice itself is also widely consumed, pressed fresh at market stalls and roadside stands. Served chilled, it is refreshing and slightly grassy, with prices around two to three euros per cup. In larger towns like Saint Denis, juice stalls can be found near the Barachois waterfront and along busy market streets, usually open from early morning until late afternoon.

For those who enjoy exploring the full range of local drinks, Creole punch is another staple. Made with rum, cane syrup, lemon juice, and sometimes a splash of bitters, it is both strong and sweet, with a taste that lingers. Most restaurants and bars serve it for around five euros, often garnished with a slice of lime. In beachside areas such as Saint Gilles les Bains, cocktails are served from late afternoon until midnight, accompanied by live music and an ocean breeze.

Coffee also plays an important role in island culture. The highlands around Cilaos produce Bourbon Pointu, a rare and delicate variety with a smooth taste and subtle acidity. Though it is among the more expensive coffees in the world, a cup in a Cilaos café costs around five to seven euros, offering travelers the chance to taste something unique to the island. Bags of roasted beans can be purchased at specialty shops or directly from plantations, usually priced from twenty to thirty euros for 250 grams.

Drinking traditions in Réunion Island carry both history and local pride. From sipping freshly pressed cane juice at a morning market to enjoying a late evening glass of rhum arrangé in a coastal bar, each experience connects visitors to the land and its people. The combination of sugarcane, fruit, and skilled craftsmanship ensures that the island's drinks are not just refreshments but cultural expressions worth exploring.

Chapter 7

Top Attractions and Natural Wonders

Piton de la Fournaise

Piton de la Fournaise is one of the most active volcanoes in the world, yet it is also one of the safest to visit thanks to careful monitoring and accessible trails. Rising more than 2600 meters above sea level on the southeastern side of Réunion Island, it is a place that draws both casual visitors and experienced hikers who want to see the raw power of nature up close. The road leading to the volcano, known as the Route du Volcan, is an attraction in itself. It begins with lush green plains and continues into a stark, almost lunar landscape as you approach the summit. The final stretch opens to Pas de Bellecombe, a large viewing area overlooking the Enclos Fouqué caldera.

Hiking is the main way to experience Piton de la Fournaise, and the most popular trail leads from Pas de Bellecombe down into the caldera and up to the rim of the main crater, Dolomieu. The round trip takes about five hours, covering roughly twelve kilometers, and is suitable for those with a moderate level of fitness. It is important to start early, both to enjoy clear skies before the afternoon mist sets in and to allow enough time to return safely before nightfall. Sturdy footwear, layered clothing, sun protection, and plenty of water are essential. Entry is free, but guided tours are available for around 40 to 60 euros per person, offering insights into geology and recent eruptions.

Access to the Pas de Bellecombe parking area is free and open daily, but weather conditions often change quickly, and roads may be closed during eruptions or heavy rain. The parking lot sits at 2311 meters and is about one hour and thirty minutes by car from Saint Pierre. Public buses do not reach this point, so renting a car or joining a tour is the most practical option.

Eruptions occur regularly, usually once every one to three years, and when conditions are safe, authorities allow visitors to view lava flows from designated areas. These events attract crowds from across the island and are announced through local tourism offices and news outlets. While access to the crater itself may be restricted during eruptions, the sight of glowing lava streaming down the slopes against the night sky is unforgettable.

For those who prefer a less strenuous experience, shorter walks around the caldera rim provide sweeping views without the long climb. Information panels at Pas de Bellecombe explain the formation of the volcano, and telescopes offer close-up views of the craters. Nearby gîtes and lodges provide overnight stays for travelers who want to begin hikes at dawn or simply enjoy the mountain atmosphere. A bed in a shared dormitory usually costs between 25 and 40 euros, while private rooms start from around 70 euros, often including breakfast.

The volcano is part of Réunion National Park, a UNESCO World Heritage site, and rangers work to protect both its natural environment and the safety of visitors. The park is open year round, though the best months for hiking are from May to November when the weather is cooler and drier. During the austral summer, from December to March, heavy rains can make trails slippery and visibility poor.

Piton de la Fournaise is more than a hiking destination. It is a living landscape that defines Réunion Island's character. Whether watching the sunrise over the caldera, tracing the hardened lava fields, or listening to stories from locals who have seen eruptions shape their homeland, the experience connects travelers with the island's most powerful natural force.

The Three Cirques

The three cirques of Réunion Island, Mafate, Cilaos and Salazie, are natural amphitheaters formed by the collapse of ancient volcanoes, each with its own landscapes, villages and character. Together they make up the heart of the island's interior, drawing hikers, photographers and travelers who want to experience life in the mountains.

Cilaos is the most accessible of the three, reached by a winding road that climbs from Saint Louis in the south. The journey itself is memorable, with hundreds of sharp bends leading to a town perched at 1200 meters. Known for its hot springs, embroidery and mountain lentils, Cilaos also produces one of the few wines grown in the Indian Ocean. The cirque is ringed by towering peaks, including Piton des Neiges, the island's highest mountain at 3070 meters. Hiking routes range from short walks through vineyards to multi day treks. The town offers a variety of accommodation, from small gîtes starting at 25 euros per night to mid range hotels charging around 80 euros for a double room. Restaurants serve local specialties, and most shops open from 9.00 to 18.00, closing for lunch between 12.00 and 14.00.

Salazie, reached from the east coast near Saint André, is the greenest of the three. Waterfalls plunge down the cliffs, the most famous being Voile de la Mariée, which cascades in thin streams across the rock face. The main village, Hell Bourg, is listed among France's most beautiful villages and is filled with colorful Creole houses. It is a good place to stay overnight, with guesthouses costing between 50 and 70 euros for a room with breakfast. Walking trails lead to viewpoints, waterfalls and forests filled with endemic plants. Markets in the village square sell fresh produce and spices, opening early in the morning until midday.

Mafate is the most remote, accessible only on foot or by helicopter, making it a paradise for hikers and those who seek isolation. The trails begin from points such as Col des Bœufs or Rivière des Galets, leading into a world of small hamlets linked only by footpaths. Accommodation comes in the form of simple gîtes, with dormitory beds from 20 euros and private rooms around 40 euros, often including meals shared with other hikers. Dinner usually consists of cari and rice, served at communal tables. The lack of road access gives Mafate a timeless feel, where the pace of life slows to the rhythm of the mountains. Shops are scarce, and most close early, so carrying supplies is essential.

Each cirque has its own atmosphere. Cilaos offers accessibility and a lively town, Salazie is lush and cultural, while Mafate is wild and cut off from the modern world. All three are part of Réunion

National Park, a UNESCO World Heritage site, and no visit to the island feels complete without spending time among these dramatic landscapes. Whether staying in a guesthouse in Hell Bourg, enjoying the hot springs in Cilaos, or waking up in a gîte deep inside Mafate, the cirques leave lasting impressions of life shaped by mountains, waterfalls and resilience.

Black and White Sand Beaches of the West Coast

The west coast of Réunion Island is lined with beaches that reflect the island's volcanic origins and tropical charm, offering both black sand shores born from lava flows and white sand stretches shaped by coral. Each has its own character, and together they form some of the island's most visited spots for swimming, sunbathing and water sports.

L'Étang Salé is the largest black sand beach on the island, located near the town of the same name about thirty minutes by car from Saint Pierre. The sand here is dark and striking, warmed quickly by the sun, and the waves attract surfers throughout the year. Swimming is possible but best enjoyed within the supervised zone patrolled by lifeguards, as currents can be strong. The beach is free to enter, parking is available, and nearby vendors sell drinks and snacks. Restaurants open from 11.00 to 21.00, offering fresh fish and Creole dishes for about 15 to 25 euros per meal.

For white sand, the lagoon beaches around Saint Gilles les Bains and La Saline les Bains are the most popular. Protected by a coral reef, the water here is calm, clear, and full of colorful fish, making it ideal for snorkeling. Plage de l'Ermitage stretches for several kilometers, shaded by casuarina trees where families picnic on weekends. Entry is free, and equipment rentals for snorkeling or stand up paddling start at 10 euros per hour from beachside kiosks. Many cafés and restaurants line the beachfront, open from morning until late evening, serving cocktails and seafood.

Boucan Canot, north of Saint Gilles, combines the drama of black volcanic rock with stretches of golden sand. It is one of the most lively beaches, with lifeguards on duty, restaurants overlooking the water, and a designated swimming area protected by nets to reduce the risk of shark encounters. Chairs and umbrellas are available for rent at around 8 to 12 euros per day, and the beach is busiest during weekends. Parking is free but fills quickly, so arriving early is recommended.

La Saline les Bains, with its shallow turquoise waters, is one of the safest spots for families. The lagoon here is wide, calm, and perfect for children. Vendors rent kayaks and pedal boats from 9.00 to 17.00, with prices starting at 15 euros. Restaurants on the sand often serve grilled fish and salads for lunch, usually between 12.00 and 14.30, while evenings are quieter.

The mix of black and white sand along the west coast creates a variety of settings, from wild stretches where waves crash against dark cliffs to peaceful lagoons where fish swim in shallow coral gardens. Spending time on these beaches is about more than relaxation, it is about enjoying the island's natural contrasts, shaped by fire and sea, and easily accessible just a short drive from the island's main towns.

Waterfalls, Rivers, and Natural Pools

Waterfalls and rivers in Réunion Island shape some of the most striking landscapes and offer refreshing places to swim or relax after hikes. The island's volcanic peaks and heavy rainfall feed countless cascades, many of which are easy to reach from main roads while others require a walk through lush valleys or mountain trails.

One of the most famous is Voile de la Mariée in Salazie, a series of thin streams running down a towering cliff, creating a veil like effect. It can be admired directly from the roadside, making it a favorite stop for travelers exploring the cirque. There is no entrance fee, parking is available nearby, and mornings are often the best time to visit before mist settles.

In the south, Grand Galet Waterfall, also known as Langevin Falls, is located near Saint Joseph. Here, multiple streams of water pour into a deep pool surrounded by greenery. The site is popular for swimming, with clear and cool water that feels rewarding after the drive along the winding Langevin River road. The area is free to enter, parking is limited but available, and local vendors often set up stalls selling fresh fruit and snacks.

Bassin la Paix near Saint Benoît offers another beautiful natural pool, shaded by basalt cliffs and surrounded by dense vegetation. It is accessible by a short but steep path, so good shoes are recommended. Swimming is common here, though visitors should be cautious of currents after heavy rains. Entry is free, and there is no set opening time, though daytime hours are best for both safety and visibility.

Closer to Saint Gilles on the west coast, Bassin des Aigrettes is a hidden gem that rewards those willing to take a short walk off the main path. The pool beneath the falls is calm and inviting, and the site remains less crowded compared to larger waterfalls. Access is free, though the trail can be slippery, so care is needed.

Cilaos, known for its mountain scenery, also has its share of natural pools along rivers such as Bras Rouge. Small cascades tumble into rocky basins where locals gather for picnics and swims. Some trails leading here begin near the village, and walks take about an hour each way. Entry is free, with marked routes that are accessible year round except during periods of heavy rain.

Many of these places are part of Réunion National Park, meaning visitors are expected to respect the environment, avoid littering, and follow safety advice. There are no entrance fees, and most sites are open throughout the day, though afternoons often bring cloud cover and sudden showers.

Waterfalls, rivers and pools are scattered across the island, giving travelers a reason to pause during drives or extend hikes into memorable excursions. Whether standing at the roadside in Salazie watching misty cascades or swimming in the clear waters of Langevin Falls, these natural settings capture the freshness and raw beauty that define Réunion's landscapes.

Botanical Gardens and Nature Parks

Botanical gardens and nature parks in Réunion Island highlight the island's extraordinary biodiversity, shaped by volcanic soil and a tropical climate. They are not just for plant lovers but for anyone who wants to see how unique species from across the Indian Ocean and beyond thrive in carefully maintained settings.

Jardin des Parfums et des Épices, located near Saint Philippe on the island's east coast, is one of the most immersive gardens. Paths wind through groves of cinnamon, nutmeg, pepper vines and tropical fruit trees, with guides explaining their uses in local cooking and medicine. Tours last around ninety minutes and cost eight euros per adult. The garden opens daily from 9.00 to 17.00, with the last entry at 16.00. It is accessible by car, and the drive along the Route des Laves adds to the experience.

Another must see is Jardin d'Eden, close to Saint Gilles les Bains. This private garden covers over two hectares and presents a mix of ornamental plants, palms and bamboo alongside medicinal herbs and local flora. Visitors can walk independently with a guidebook, making it a relaxed experience. Entry costs eight euros for adults and four euros for children, and the garden is open daily from 10.00 to 18.00. Its location near the beaches makes it easy to combine with a day by the sea.

Conservatoire Botanique National de Mascarin, set in the hills above Saint Leu, focuses on conservation and education. The park protects many endangered plant species from the Mascarenes, a group of islands that includes Réunion, Mauritius and Rodrigues. The grounds are spread across historic estate land with terraces overlooking the ocean. Admission is seven euros for adults, with reduced prices for children and students. Opening hours run from Tuesday to Sunday, 9.00 to 17.00. Guided tours and exhibitions add depth, making it both beautiful and informative.

Réunion National Park itself can be considered a vast natural garden, covering more than forty percent of the island and recognized as a UNESCO World Heritage site. Trails pass through forests filled with tree ferns, orchids and endemic species found nowhere else. Access is free, though guided tours with park rangers are available at different visitor centers, usually costing from fifteen to twenty euros.

The park is open year round, though weather conditions can affect accessibility to certain trails.

Smaller village gardens also carry cultural value. In Hell Bourg, visitors can walk through Creole house gardens where medicinal herbs, fruit trees and flowers are planted in traditional style. Entry fees are usually symbolic, around two to three euros, and they give a sense of how people once lived in harmony with the land.

Botanical gardens and nature parks offer a slower way to experience Réunion Island, away from the energy of the coasts and mountains. Whether strolling among spice trees, learning about rare orchids, or sitting beneath bamboo groves, these places connect visitors with the island's living heritage in a calm and welcoming setting.

Chapter 8

Outdoor Adventures and Activities

Hiking Trails for All Levels

Hiking in Réunion Island offers something for every traveler, from short walks through forests to multi day adventures across volcanic peaks. The island's varied landscapes make it one of the best places for outdoor exploration, and trails are well marked thanks to Réunion's inclusion in France's national hiking network.

For beginners or those seeking a gentle introduction, the walk to Bassin Vital near Saint Paul is an easy path that takes less than an hour round trip. The trail leads through lush vegetation to a natural pool where locals swim. Access is free, parking is nearby, and mornings are often the most pleasant time to visit before the heat builds. Another easy route is the coastal path around Saint Leu, where the trail follows the shoreline with views of the lagoon. It is flat, open all day, and ideal for families.

Moderate hikes are plentiful, with one of the most rewarding being the route to Roche Merveilleuse in Cilaos. It takes about two hours and offers panoramic views of the cirque and surrounding peaks. The trail begins near the town and is accessible without special permits. Entry is free, and it is possible to combine the hike with a visit to local shops and cafés in Cilaos afterward. Salazie also provides good mid level trails, including paths leading to Voile de la Mariée waterfall. Walks here usually last two to three hours and pass through small villages and farmland.

For those ready for more challenging hikes, Mafate delivers a truly remote experience. With no road access, all trails lead into a world of isolated hamlets connected only by footpaths. Routes such as Col des Bœufs to Marla or Rivière des Galets to Roche Plate take between five and seven hours, with steep climbs and descents. Hikers stay overnight in gîtes, where dormitory beds cost from 20 to 25 euros per night including meals. Trails are open year round, though they are best enjoyed during the dry season from May to November.

The most demanding routes are found on Piton des Neiges, the highest peak on the island. The climb usually begins from Cilaos or Hell Bourg, with hikers starting in the early hours of the morning to reach the summit for sunrise. The trek takes about six to eight hours round trip, depending on the chosen route, and requires good fitness and proper gear. Many hikers spend the night at the mountain refuge, Gîte de la Caverne Dufour, where beds cost about 25 euros and dinner is available for an additional 20 euros. Reservations are recommended, and the refuge is open year round.

Piton de la Fournaise, one of the world's most active volcanoes, also offers dramatic hiking. The trail from Pas de Bellecombe to the Dolomieu crater rim is about twelve kilometers and takes five hours, crossing lava fields and offering views into the vast caldera. Entry is free, but conditions can change quickly, and the route is sometimes closed during eruptions. Parking at Pas de Bellecombe is free, and tours with guides cost from 40 to 60 euros per person.

No matter the level of difficulty, hikers should carry enough water, snacks, and sun protection, as well as clothing for changing weather. Trails are open without entrance fees, but safety depends on preparation and respect for conditions. From short family walks to climbs above 3000 meters, Réunion's hiking network ensures that every visitor can find a path suited to their pace, with landscapes that always reward the effort.

Paragliding and Aerial Views of the Island

Paragliding in Réunion Island is one of the most exhilarating ways to experience the island's landscapes, giving travelers the chance to see lagoons, cirques and volcanic slopes from above. The most popular spot for takeoff is in the hills above Saint Leu on the west coast, where favorable winds and open skies create ideal flying conditions. From here, flights descend toward the lagoon, offering sweeping views of coral reefs, villages and mountains stretching into the distance.

Tandem paragliding is accessible to beginners, as a professional pilot controls the flight while the passenger simply enjoys the view. Companies such as Air Réunion and Parapente Réunion offer flights starting at around 90 euros for twenty to thirty minutes in the air. Longer flights lasting up to an hour cost between 120 and 150 euros, and packages with in flight photos and videos are usually available for an additional 20 euros. Takeoffs generally operate between 8.00 and 16.00, when wind conditions are most reliable.

For those who want a higher perspective, helicopter tours from Saint Gilles les Bains or Saint Pierre provide aerial views of the island's most dramatic sites. Flights often pass over Piton de la Fournaise, the Cirque de Mafate, and waterfalls hidden deep in valleys. Prices start from 240 euros per person for a twenty minute flight, rising to around 400 euros for longer circuits of fifty minutes covering the volcano, cirques and lagoon. Most companies operate daily from

7.00 to 17.00, weather permitting, and advance booking is recommended.

Ultralight flights are another option, offering a more intimate experience in small aircraft with open cockpits. Departing from Pierrefonds Airport near Saint Pierre, these flights last about thirty minutes and cost around 130 euros per person. The sensation is different from paragliding or helicopters, with the slower pace allowing travelers to fully appreciate the scenery below.

The island's varied landscapes make every aerial adventure unique. On clear mornings, the views stretch from the coastline to the highest peaks, and in some seasons, whales can even be spotted in the waters offshore. Operators prioritize safety, with certified pilots and weather checks before every flight, but conditions can shift quickly, so flexibility with timing is important.

Paragliding and aerial excursions add a perspective that hiking or driving cannot provide. Floating silently above a lagoon or circling the rim of a volcano brings a sense of freedom that leaves lasting memories. It is one of the most rewarding activities in Réunion Island for those who want to experience both thrill and beauty in a single moment.

Scuba Diving, Snorkeling, and Marine Life

Scuba diving and snorkeling in Réunion Island reveal a side of the island that is as captivating as its mountains and volcanoes. The west coast, protected by a coral reef stretching from Saint Gilles to Saint Leu, provides calm waters, clear visibility and an abundance of marine life. Parrotfish, butterflyfish and angelfish glide among coral gardens, while sea turtles are often spotted near the reef edges.

Snorkeling is the easiest way to experience this underwater world. The lagoon at L'Ermitage is the most popular spot, with shallow, calm waters that are safe even for beginners and children. Equipment can be rented from beach kiosks for around 10 euros per hour, and guided snorkeling tours with local instructors cost between 20 and 30 euros. These tours often include explanations of the reef's ecosystem and are available daily from 9.00 to 16.00.

For scuba diving, centers in Saint Gilles les Bains, Saint Leu and Étang Salé offer courses and excursions throughout the year. A beginner's introduction, often called a baptism dive, costs around 60 euros and takes place at depths of six to ten meters with an instructor. Certified divers can join boat trips to explore sites such as Cap La Houssaye, with its rocky slopes covered in coral, or the marine reserve near Saint Paul, where larger species like barracuda and rays can be encountered. Prices for two tank dives usually range from 80 to 100 euros, including equipment. Most centers operate daily from 7.30 to 17.00, with morning departures offering the best conditions.

During the cooler months from June to September, humpback whales migrate near Réunion's shores. While diving with them is not permitted, many operators combine snorkeling with whale watching tours, giving travelers the chance to observe these giants from the surface. Tours last around three hours, cost about 70 euros per person, and depart from marinas in Saint Gilles or Saint Leu.

Safety is a priority, as some areas outside the reef are prone to strong currents and shark risks. This is why organized trips with licensed operators are recommended. Within the lagoons, conditions remain calm, making snorkeling both safe and rewarding.

Marine life in Réunion is vibrant and varied, from tiny reef fish to dolphins and sea turtles. Every outing offers a chance to encounter something new, whether exploring shallow coral gardens with a mask and snorkel or descending into deeper waters on a scuba trip. The experience adds a different dimension to a stay on the island, combining adventure with quiet moments of wonder beneath the surface.

Whale Watching and Dolphin Tours

Whale watching and dolphin tours in Réunion Island have become one of the island's most memorable experiences, offering the chance to see marine life in its natural habitat while cruising along the west coast. From June to September, humpback whales migrate through the waters near the island, coming close to the surface as they breach, slap their tails and care for their calves. Dolphins can be spotted year round, often swimming alongside boats in playful groups.

Tours depart mainly from marinas in Saint Gilles les Bains, Saint Leu and sometimes Saint Pierre. They usually last two to three hours, with morning departures being the most popular as the sea is calmer. Prices start at around 45 euros per person for a dolphin tour and between 55 and 70 euros for a combined whale and dolphin outing. Children's tickets are often discounted, usually costing about 30 euros. Boats operate daily during the season, typically between 7.00 and 16.00, with departures every few hours depending on demand and sea conditions.

Operators are careful to follow strict codes of conduct to avoid disturbing the animals. Boats maintain a safe distance, engines are slowed when pods are near, and the focus is on observation rather than chasing. Many tours are led by guides who explain whale and dolphin behavior, making the experience both entertaining and educational. Some companies also use hydrophones to let passengers hear the haunting songs of the whales, adding an unforgettable element to the outing.

During the off season for whales, dolphin tours remain a highlight. Spinner dolphins are the most common, easily recognized by their acrobatic leaps. Pantropical spotted dolphins and bottlenose dolphins are also frequently seen. Watching them swim in pods against the backdrop of volcanic cliffs or calm lagoons shows another side of the island's diverse natural environment.

Whale watching season aligns well with the cooler, drier months, making it an ideal time to combine these tours with hiking or exploring the mountains. As tours depend heavily on weather, it is best to book early in a trip and stay flexible, as strong winds or rough seas can lead to cancellations.

Whether spotting a humpback whale breaching offshore or following a pod of dolphins gliding effortlessly beside the boat, these excursions add a sense of wonder to a visit. They connect travelers with the wild beauty of Réunion Island in a way that stays with them long after the boat returns to port.

Canyoning and Mountain Sports

Canyoning and mountain sports in Réunion Island show the wilder side of its landscapes, drawing adventure seekers into deep gorges, basalt cliffs and steep ravines carved by water over centuries. Few destinations offer such variety within such a small area, and the island has become one of the premier spots in the world for these activities.

Canyoning is available in different locations suited to all levels. Beginners often start in Langevin or Fleurs Jaunes near Cilaos, where short descents, natural slides and small abseils introduce the thrill without being overwhelming. These half day outings usually cost around 55 to 70 euros per person, with equipment and a certified guide included. For those looking for something more demanding, Takamaka on the east side of the island offers some of the most technical canyoning in the world. It involves long rappels down waterfalls, swims through narrow gorges and climbs across slippery rock faces. These full day excursions are priced between 90 and 120 euros and require a good level of fitness.

Tours typically run daily from 8.00 to 16.00, though weather conditions often dictate schedules since heavy rain can quickly raise river levels. Operators provide wetsuits, harnesses and helmets, and group sizes are usually small to maintain safety. Most guides are bilingual, offering explanations in French and English, and photos or videos of the descent can often be purchased for an extra 10 to 20 euros.

Beyond canyoning, mountain sports in Réunion include climbing, mountain biking and trail running. The volcanic slopes around Cilaos are well known for climbing routes, from easier walls suited to beginners to advanced multi pitch climbs on basalt cliffs. Equipment rental and a half day guided climb usually cost about 60 euros. Mountain biking is another popular choice, with descents starting high above Maïdo and winding down toward the coast. Tours last four to five hours, cost around 65 euros including bike and safety gear, and depart daily in the morning.

The island is also a destination for trail running, with events such as the Grand Raid drawing participants from around the world. Even for non competitors, marked trails allow visitors to test their endurance on steep ascents and rocky paths, with views of cirques and volcanic landscapes as the reward.

All of these activities highlight the rugged beauty of Réunion Island and the need to respect its natural forces. Conditions change quickly in the mountains, so booking with licensed guides ensures both safety and local knowledge. Whether sliding down a cool canyon stream or pushing up a volcanic ridge, the island's mountains provide challenges that leave travelers with stories as striking as the scenery itself.

Chapter 9

Shopping, Entertainment, and Nightlife

Souvenir Shopping and Local Handicrafts

Souvenir shopping in Réunion Island brings together the island's cultural mix and its natural richness, offering travelers keepsakes that carry the spirit of the place. Markets and small shops across towns and villages are filled with handicrafts, local food products and artisanal creations that make for meaningful gifts and reminders of a trip.

The covered market in Saint Paul, open on Fridays and Saturdays from 7.00 to 18.00, is one of the best spots to browse. Stalls are packed with colorful sarongs, woven baskets, hand carved wooden masks and jars of homemade jams flavored with mango, passion fruit or guava. Spices sold in small packets are popular purchases, with vanilla pods among the most sought after. Prices vary, but a bundle of locally grown vanilla can cost between 15 and 25 euros depending on quality, while hand woven baskets start from around 10 euros.

In Saint Denis, the capital, the Grand Marché offers a similar experience with a slightly more urban atmosphere. Here, travelers can find artisanal soaps made with essential oils from island plants, embroidered textiles and decorative items crafted by local artisans. The market is open daily from 7.00 to 17.00 and is conveniently located near the city center.

For a more personal touch, villages in the cirques often sell unique items not found elsewhere. In Cilaos, embroidery is a tradition that dates back generations, with finely worked linens and tablecloths displayed in small workshops. Prices depend on the detail of the work but generally range from 20 euros for smaller pieces to over 100 euros for larger items. In Salazie, baskets woven from vacoa leaves are sold at roadside stalls, each piece practical and sturdy, reflecting everyday island life.

Artisan boutiques in coastal towns also stock rum infused with spices, locally roasted coffee and chocolate made from beans grown in the region. A bottle of spiced rum can cost around 20 euros, while a pack of roasted coffee is usually about 8 to 10 euros. Many shops are open from 9.00 to 18.00, closing briefly in the middle of the day.

Buying handicrafts supports small businesses and keeps traditional practices alive. The variety of items, from handmade jewelry using volcanic rock to vibrant paintings inspired by Creole culture, ensures that there is something for every taste and budget. Browsing these markets and shops is not just about purchasing souvenirs but also about connecting with the island's creativity and heritage. Each item carries a story, making it more than just a gift but a memory tied to Réunion Island itself.

Colorful Markets and What to Buy

Markets in Réunion Island are more than just shopping venues, they are lively spaces where the island's culture, flavors and traditions come together. The weekly market in Saint Paul is the largest and perhaps the most atmospheric, spreading out near the seafront every Friday and Saturday from 7.00 until 18.00. Rows of stalls overflow with tropical fruits such as lychees, mangoes and pineapples, while tables stacked with spices fill the air with the aroma of cinnamon, turmeric and cloves. Vanilla, one of the island's prized exports, is sold in bundles, with prices starting around 15 euros depending on quality.

Beyond fresh produce, Saint Paul's market is also the place to buy handmade crafts, woven baskets, and vibrant sarongs known locally as paréos. Many of these textiles feature bold floral designs in bright colors, and they are both inexpensive and practical, usually costing around 10 to 20 euros. For those looking for gifts, stalls offer jars of jam flavored with guava, passion fruit or papaya, often priced at about 5 to 8 euros each.

The Grand Marché in Saint Denis, open daily from 7.00 to 17.00, provides a more permanent version of this experience. Located in the capital, it is a good spot for visitors who cannot make it to the weekly events. Here, shoppers can find artisanal soaps made from essential oils, decorative items carved from wood and jewelry crafted with volcanic rock. The market has a mix of stalls selling affordable souvenirs and higher end items reflecting the island's diverse influences.

In Cilaos, a visit to the local market offers something different, with embroidery and lacework still made using traditional techniques. These pieces are sold directly by artisans, and while smaller works can be found for 20 euros, larger tablecloths or bed linens often exceed 100 euros. In Salazie, baskets woven from vacoa leaves are common, prized for both their durability and their link to local heritage.

Food markets are equally rewarding. At Le Chaudron market near Saint Denis, held on Wednesdays and Sundays from early morning until around 13.00, locals stock up on vegetables, fresh herbs, and prepared snacks. Street food vendors add to the buzz, selling samosas, bouchons and sweet fritters that can be eaten on the go for just a couple of euros.

Visiting markets in Réunion Island is not just about what you buy but also the experience of mingling with residents, hearing Creole spoken alongside French, and taking in the colors and scents. Whether it is a bag of fresh spices, a handmade basket, or a piece of embroidery, the purchase comes with the memory of the setting in which it was found, giving every souvenir a story tied to the island.

Shopping Centers and Modern Boutiques

Shopping in Réunion Island is not only about lively markets and handicrafts, as modern shopping centers and boutiques also offer a wide range of experiences. For those who prefer structured environments with international brands, climate control and convenient facilities, the island's malls are the place to go.

Jumbo Score Sainte Marie, near Roland Garros Airport, is one of the largest shopping complexes. It combines a hypermarket with a selection of fashion outlets, bookstores, electronics and food courts. Open daily from 9.00 to 20.00, it is especially useful for travelers stopping on their way to or from the airport. Prices align closely with those in mainland France, though special offers and seasonal sales provide good deals.

In Saint Denis, the Duparc shopping center has become a favorite for both locals and visitors. Open from 9.30 to 19.30 Monday to

Saturday, it offers clothing shops, beauty stores and small cafés for a break between browsing. Boutiques here often blend international labels with French and Creole inspired collections, giving shoppers the chance to find something unique while still having access to familiar global names.

South of the island, Le Port's Cap Sacré Cœur stands out with its mix of high street fashion, sports stores and a cinema. Open from 9.30 to 19.30 Monday to Saturday, it attracts families as much as fashion hunters, and seasonal events or promotions often add to the lively atmosphere. Clothing ranges from casual beachwear to elegant evening outfits, with mid range pricing that makes it accessible to a wide audience.

Boutiques outside the malls have their own appeal, especially in towns such as Saint Gilles les Bains or Saint Pierre. Small independent shops showcase beach fashion, jewelry made with volcanic stone or shells, and interior décor blending local materials with contemporary design. Many open from 10.00 to 18.00, often closing for lunch between 12.30 and 14.00. Prices vary widely, with handcrafted jewelry starting at around 15 euros and upscale fashion pieces climbing into the hundreds.

For those looking for souvenirs with a polished finish, designer boutiques often carry high quality rum, artisanal chocolates and fine vanilla presented in stylish packaging. These shops cater to both gift buyers and those who want to take home luxury goods with a strong sense of place.

Shopping centers and modern boutiques in Réunion Island balance convenience with variety. They are practical stops for travelers in need of essentials, while also providing stylish options and contemporary flair. Combined with the island's markets, they round out the shopping experience, offering something for both bargain seekers and those after refined purchases.

Nightlife in Saint Gilles and Saint Denis

Nightlife in Réunion Island has two distinct flavors, and they are best experienced in Saint Gilles on the west coast and Saint Denis in the north. Saint Gilles is the heart of the island's beachside energy, where evenings often start with cocktails along the seafront before moving into lively bars and clubs. Many establishments are concentrated near the marina, making it easy to hop from one place to another without worrying about long distances. Popular spots open around 18.00 and keep going until 2.00 in the morning on weekends. Prices vary depending on the venue, but a cocktail usually costs between 7 and 12 euros, while entrance to clubs can range from free to 15 euros depending on the event.

Live music is part of the scene, with bars featuring local bands playing maloya and sega alongside international covers. On weekends, clubs such as Le Cubana or Les Paillotes attract a younger crowd with DJs mixing everything from electronic beats to Latin rhythms. Many places also serve light food late into the night, often Creole dishes or tapas style snacks, giving the evening a social, relaxed feel.

In contrast, Saint Denis offers a more cosmopolitan night out. As the capital, it has cocktail lounges, cultural venues and a handful of trendy clubs. Rooftop bars and lounges around the city center give travelers a more polished experience, often open until 1.00 during the week and later on Fridays and Saturdays. Prices are similar to those in Saint Gilles, with a glass of wine averaging 5 euros and more elaborate cocktails going for around 10 euros.

For those who enjoy cultural evenings, Saint Denis also has theaters and performance spaces where concerts and shows run into the night. These venues add a different dimension to the city's nightlife, combining entertainment with insight into the island's music and traditions.

Both towns cater to different moods. Saint Gilles thrives on its resort atmosphere, lively and open air, with the ocean never far away. Saint Denis appeals with its urban setting, stylish venues and broader mix of cultural offerings. Together they show that nights in Réunion Island can be as vibrant as the days, offering visitors a chance to experience the island's social energy after the sun goes down.

Cultural Shows and Sega Music Nights

Cultural shows and sega music nights in Réunion Island are evenings filled with rhythm, storytelling and communal spirit. Sega, often performed barefoot on sand or grass, is more than music; it is a living tradition that blends African, Malagasy and European influences. The songs are carried by drums, triangles, and the roulèr, a large drum that provides the heartbeat of the performance. The melodies are both joyful and nostalgic, and the dances that accompany them are fluid, with swaying hips and expressive gestures that captivate visitors and locals alike.

In Saint Gilles les Bains, beachside restaurants and bars frequently host sega evenings where musicians play live while diners enjoy Creole food. These events usually begin around 20.00 and continue until midnight. Many are free for those eating at the restaurant, while standalone shows charge an entry fee ranging from 10 to 20 euros. Some venues also offer set menus that pair local dishes such as cari poulet or rougail saucisse with the performance, usually priced around 25 to 35 euros.

In Saint Denis, cultural centers and open air festivals often feature sega nights as part of their programming. The Théâtre de Champ Fleuri occasionally hosts larger events where professional groups bring a more polished version of the tradition, often accompanied by modern choreography. Tickets for these performances usually cost between 15 and 30 euros depending on seating. Smaller venues in the capital, on the other hand, keep things intimate with casual gatherings where audiences are encouraged to join the dancing.

In towns such as Saint Pierre or Cilaos, sega nights are part of local celebrations and can take place in village squares, especially during festivals. These are usually free and open to everyone, making them an ideal way for travelers to feel the island's community spirit. Drinks and snacks are often sold at nearby stalls, adding to the festive air.

What makes sega nights memorable is not only the music but also the shared atmosphere. Visitors are rarely left sitting for long, as locals often invite newcomers to join the circle of dancers. The combination of live percussion, spirited voices and spontaneous movement creates an experience that feels both welcoming and unforgettable. Cultural shows and sega nights are one of the most authentic ways to connect with Réunion Island, giving travelers a lasting impression of its soul after the sun goes down.

Chapter 10

Practical Tips for a Smooth Stay

Internet, Mobile Service, and Staying Connected

Staying connected in Réunion Island is straightforward, as the territory follows the French system for telecommunications. Mobile coverage is reliable across cities and coastal towns, with most rural areas and mountain villages also well served, though signal strength can dip in deep valleys or remote hiking spots. The main providers are Orange, SFR, Free and Zeop, all of which offer prepaid SIM cards that can be purchased at airports, shopping centers and official stores. Prices for SIM cards begin at around 10 euros, with data packages starting from 15 euros for a few gigabytes valid for one month. Stores generally open from 9.00 to 18.00 Monday through Saturday, with larger outlets in malls often extending hours until 20.00.

Wi Fi is widely available in hotels, guesthouses and most modern cafés. Many accommodations provide it free of charge, though some budget lodgings may limit speed or ask for a small daily fee of around 2 to 5 euros. Restaurants in Saint Denis and Saint Gilles often include free Wi Fi access for customers, making it easy to check maps or send messages while enjoying a meal. For travelers needing steady connections, coworking spaces in Saint Denis such as Le Transfo offer high speed access, with day passes priced around 15 euros and monthly rates available for longer stays.

International roaming works in Réunion Island, but costs are usually high unless the visitor already has a French or European Union mobile plan, which often extends seamlessly to Réunion without extra charges. For non EU visitors, buying a local SIM card is almost always more economical. Mobile data is fast, with 4G widely available and 5G expanding in larger towns.

Public spaces such as Roland Garros Airport and major shopping centers also provide free Wi Fi, though speeds can vary depending on the number of users. Internet cafés, once common, are now rare, replaced by better mobile data coverage and more accessible public Wi Fi points.

For calls within Réunion Island, standard mobile rates apply, while international calls to Africa, Asia or the Americas can be costly. Many visitors rely on internet based services for communication back home, taking advantage of the solid broadband network.

Overall, staying connected on the island is convenient and affordable. Whether arranging tours, uploading photos of volcanic peaks, or keeping in touch with family abroad, travelers will find reliable options that make it easy to stay online throughout their stay.

Public Holidays and How They Affect Travel

Public holidays in Réunion Island follow the French calendar with a few additions that reflect the island's unique cultural history, and they can influence the way travelers plan their days. On these dates, government offices, banks and many shops remain closed, while public transportation runs on reduced schedules. Larger supermarkets and shopping centers in Saint Denis or Saint Pierre sometimes open for a few hours in the morning but smaller stores usually shut for the entire day.

Fixed French holidays such as New Year's Day on January 1, Bastille Day on July 14 and Christmas on December 25 are observed, and during these days restaurants and attractions in popular tourist towns may stay open but with shorter hours. Some establishments raise prices slightly on holiday evenings, especially in restaurants that include special menus. Expect to pay around 30 to 40 euros for a fixed course dinner when a normal day's menu might cost 20 to 25 euros.

Unique to Réunion is the celebration of Abolition of Slavery Day on December 20, known locally as Fèt Kaf. This is one of the island's most important cultural events, marked with music, dance and community gatherings. On this day, most offices and schools close, but the streets fill with celebrations, particularly in Saint Denis and Saint Paul, where sega and maloya performances continue late into the night. Travelers visiting during this period should plan ahead as buses may run less frequently and taxis can be in high demand.

Religious festivals also affect daily life. Easter, All Saints' Day on November 1 and Assumption on August 15 are Catholic holidays when many families gather for church services. Hindu festivals, especially Cavadee and Dipavali, though not official public holidays, also bring processions and closures in certain neighborhoods. These create rich opportunities for visitors to witness cultural traditions but can cause traffic congestion and occasional delays in public services.

During holidays linked to the school calendar, such as late December to early January and late July to mid August, popular coastal resorts like Saint Gilles are crowded. Hotels and guesthouses fill quickly and prices for accommodations rise by 20 to 30 percent compared to the low season. Rental cars, normally available from 25 euros per day, can climb to 40 euros or more during these periods.

Travelers who are flexible can use these holidays to their advantage. National celebrations often include free concerts, parades or public fireworks, giving visitors a lively way to experience local culture. At the same time, it is wise to stock up on essentials a day before major holidays, as grocery stores and bakeries may not reopen until the following day.

Understanding the rhythm of public holidays ensures smoother travel. While they may bring temporary closures or reduced schedules, they also offer windows into the island's cultural soul, where music, food and tradition come together in ways that are worth adjusting plans for.

Budgeting and Average Daily Costs

Traveling through Réunion Island can be tailored to suit different budgets, but it helps to understand what an average day's expenses look like. For those keeping costs low, guesthouses and basic gîtes in smaller towns or villages are available from around 35 euros per night. Mid range travelers booking hotels in coastal towns like Saint Gilles or Saint Pierre should plan for 70 to 120 euros per night, while luxury resorts with pools and beachfront settings can easily reach 200 euros and above.

Food is another area where daily spending varies. A simple Creole meal at a local snack bar often costs 7 to 10 euros, while dining in a casual restaurant with table service usually ranges between 15 and 25 euros per person. For fine dining, especially in French influenced restaurants in Saint Denis, a set menu can reach 50 euros or more.

Street food such as samosas or bonbons piments are affordable, often less than 2 euros each, making them a popular choice for quick bites.

Transportation is affordable for those using buses, where fares are about 2 euros per trip. However, routes are limited and less frequent in the evenings, so many visitors opt for car rentals. Daily rates start at 25 euros for compact vehicles, but prices rise during school holidays. Petrol is controlled across the island, with prices similar to mainland France, usually around 1.70 to 1.80 euros per liter. Parking in towns often requires a small fee of 1 to 2 euros per hour, though coastal villages sometimes allow free spaces near beaches.

Activities can add to the budget depending on interests. Guided hikes in the cirques or around Piton de la Fournaise usually start at 40 euros per person, while paragliding in Saint Leu is about 80 to 100 euros for a tandem flight. Whale watching or dolphin tours cost between 50 and 70 euros for half a day. Entrance to most natural attractions is free, including waterfalls and beaches, but botanical gardens and cultural sites may charge around 5 to 10 euros per ticket.

Daily costs for a budget traveler staying in guesthouses, eating local food and using buses average around 50 to 60 euros. A mid range traveler combining hotel stays, restaurant meals and some guided activities should expect to spend 120 to 150 euros per day. For those choosing resorts, fine dining and adventure sports, daily spending can exceed 250 euros.

Shops and supermarkets generally open from 8.00 to 19.00, Monday through Saturday, though some close midday for a couple of hours.

Larger malls remain open until 20.00, making it easy to stock up on snacks or supplies without interrupting daily plans.

Managing expenses on the island is straightforward once visitors balance accommodation, meals and activities according to their preferences. Whether traveling on a modest budget or seeking comfort and luxury, the island offers clear options that make it possible to plan without surprises.

Accessibility for Travelers with Disabilities

Travelers with disabilities will find that Réunion Island has made progress in improving accessibility, though conditions vary between urban centers and natural areas. In the capital, Saint Denis, sidewalks are wider and newer public buildings provide ramps and lifts, making it easier to move around. Hotels in the mid range and luxury categories often include accessible rooms with roll in showers, and staff are generally attentive to guests who need additional support. Smaller family run guesthouses may not always have adapted facilities, so it is best to confirm in advance before booking.

Roland Garros Airport in Saint Denis is equipped with assistance services for reduced mobility passengers. Trained staff are available to help from check in through boarding, and wheelchairs can be requested ahead of time. The airport also has accessible restrooms and designated parking spaces near the entrance. Flights arriving from Paris, Marseille and Lyon with Air France, Air Austral and Corsair offer the option to book assistance at no extra charge.

Public buses on the island are a mixed experience. Newer vehicles in larger towns like Saint Denis and Saint Pierre are fitted with low floors and designated spaces for wheelchairs, but in rural routes older buses still operate without these adaptations. Bus tickets remain inexpensive at around 2 euros, and drivers are generally supportive, though boarding can be slow on older vehicles. For travelers who need reliable accessibility, private transfers or adapted taxis are often the more comfortable choice.

Car rental agencies in Saint Denis and Saint Gilles provide vehicles with automatic transmission, though fully adapted cars with hand controls are limited. Booking early is advisable, especially during the school holiday months when demand rises. Parking spaces reserved for people with disabilities are marked clearly in city centers, shopping malls and airports, and they are regularly monitored to prevent misuse.

Natural attractions remain more challenging, as the rugged volcanic landscapes are not always adapted for wheelchair access. However, several sites have made improvements. The Jardin de l'État in Saint Denis has paved pathways and shaded seating, with free entry daily between 9.00 and 18.00. Some coastal promenades in Saint Gilles are flat and well maintained, making them suitable for wheelchairs. Viewing platforms at popular spots such as waterfalls or lookouts occasionally have ramps, though trails leading into the cirques or up to Piton de la Fournaise are generally not accessible without assistance.

Medical services are reliable, with hospitals in Saint Denis and Saint Pierre offering modern facilities. Pharmacies are widespread and staff are accustomed to advising travelers. Emergency services can be reached by dialing 15, and many hospitals provide interpreters or multilingual staff to assist foreign visitors.

Travelers with disabilities will find that Réunion is steadily improving in terms of accessible tourism, though some limitations remain in the wilder parts of the island. With advance planning, especially in arranging accommodation and transfers, it is possible to enjoy the island's culture, food and coastal beauty without unnecessary difficulty.

Departure Tips and Last-minute Essentials

Preparing for departure from Réunion Island is easier when you allow yourself enough time at the airport and take care of small essentials before leaving your accommodation. Roland Garros Airport in Saint Denis is the main international gateway, and travelers are advised to arrive at least three hours before long haul flights and two hours before regional departures. Security checks can move quickly, but queues form during the busy morning and evening rush when flights to Paris and nearby islands take off almost back to back.

Duty free shops at the airport sell rum, vanilla, coffee and spices, all popular souvenirs, but prices are higher than at markets in town. If you prefer shopping before reaching the airport, the Saint Denis covered market and the Saint Paul open air market are excellent spots for stocking up on last minute items. The Saint Denis market is open daily except Sunday from 6.00 to 17.00, while the Saint Paul market is busiest on Fridays and Saturdays from 6.00 to 18.00. These markets accept cash and cards, but it is wise to carry some euros in smaller notes for quicker transactions.

Pharmacies near the airport in Sainte Marie are open from 8.30 to 19.00 Monday to Saturday, offering any medication or travel sized health supplies you may need. For urgent needs outside regular hours, one pharmacy in each district rotates as the on duty pharmacy and will display its schedule on local listings. Supermarkets such as Carrefour and Score, open from 8.30 to 20.00, are good places to buy snacks, water or last minute toiletries.

If you rented a car, allow additional time to refuel before returning the vehicle. Most rental companies require the tank to be full, and the nearest petrol stations to the airport are in Sainte Marie along the RN2 road. Petrol stations generally operate from 6.00 to 20.00, though automated pumps that accept credit cards remain open 24 hours.

Travelers should double check baggage allowances with their airline, especially on regional carriers where weight limits may be stricter. Air Austral, for example, often sets a lower allowance on inter island routes compared to flights to France. Oversized luggage such as surfboards or hiking equipment should be declared in advance to avoid delays.

Finally, keep aside a small amount of cash for any airport extras such as snacks, luggage wrapping services or a final drink at the café before boarding. Taxis to Roland Garros Airport from central Saint Denis cost around 20 to 25 euros during the day, with higher fares at night. Shuttles and hotel transfers should be booked at least a day in advance to guarantee timely arrival. With these details handled early, the departure process becomes smooth, leaving you with a calm ending to your stay on the island.

Conclusion

Every journey to Réunion Island leaves travelers with something unforgettable, whether it is the thrill of standing at the rim of Piton de la Fournaise, the quiet beauty of walking through lush cirques, or the warmth of a meal shared in a Creole kitchen. This guide has given you the tools to plan with ease, move around confidently, and embrace the many layers of the island's culture, landscapes, and traditions. From navigating public transport to tasting street food at local markets, from choosing the right place to stay to respecting the customs that shape daily life, you now have a complete companion to make the most of your time here.

What sets Réunion apart is not just the dramatic scenery or the blend of French and Creole heritage, but the way it rewards those who are curious and willing to experience it fully. Every waterfall, mountain ridge, or small village carries its own story, and by following the paths laid out in these pages, you will discover them in ways that feel personal and lasting.

As you return home, the memories of island sunsets, Sega rhythms, and market spices will stay with you, reminding you that this corner of the Indian Ocean is more than a destination. It is an encounter with nature at its most powerful and culture at its most welcoming. Let this guide inspire you to explore with respect, savor every detail, and carry a piece of Réunion with you long after your plane takes off.

Your adventure does not end when you leave. It becomes a part of your own story, ready to be told, shared, and perhaps lived again when you choose to return.

Printed in Dunstable, United Kingdom